Altered Images

Becoming parents of our disabled children

Edited by

Libby Fletcher
Rebecca O'Rourke
Gillian Payne
Heidi Ridgewell
Sue Smith
Gillian Upton Holmes

With contributions and assistance from

A Mum
Anonymous
A Young Person
Lesley
John Smith
Abbi Ward

This book is dedicated to all our children, and all your children.

Ryedale Special Families
121 Town Street
Old Malton
Malton
North Yorkshire
YO17 7HD
United Kingdom

We gratefully acknowledge financial support from

The Charles and Elsie Sykes Trust
North Yorkshire County Council (Ryedale Area Committee)
North Yorkshire Health Authority (Health Improvement Programme)

ISBN-10: 0 9552146 0 2
ISBN-13: 978 0 9552146 0 8

First published in 2006 by Ryedale Special Families

Cover design by yo-yo.uk.com, York

Page layout, printed and distributed by:
York Publishing Services Ltd
64 Hallfield Road
Layerthorpe
York
YO31 7ZQ
Tel: 01904 431213; Fax: 01904 430868; Website: www.yps-publishing.co.uk

Contents

Preface

Long ago when I was the local 'school doctor' in this lovely part of North Yorkshire I was invited to have coffee with a small group of parents of children with special needs. None of us realised then that this was to lead to the formation of the parents support group that came to be Ryedale Special Families. RSF is different from many groups in two respects. It is owned and led by parents and it supports parents whose children have a wide range of disabilities.

I was intrigued when I heard that some of the parents in RSF had formed a writing group, which has led to the publication of their work. Reading *Altered Images* has been both pleasurable and painful, for this is a hard-hitting book.

A few pages in and I felt a forcible blow to my solar plexus as I was gripped by the depth and intensity of feeling transmitted from its pages. I forwarded it to my administrator Gilly to print from the computer. When I saw her later in the week she said 'I couldn't help reading some of it and it hit me just here' – indicating the lower end of her sternum. When I was at medical school this area was referred to as the solar plexus. It is described anatomically as a network of autonomic nerves. Yesterday, I looked it up in a medical dictionary, which referred to it as the 'abdominal brain'. This writing strikes that part – the seat of deep emotion. It deserves to be read by all who are in contact with parents of children with special needs. Why? Because they will either be parents who recognise their experiences on its pages or professionals who will find their 'abdominal brain' awakes. It gives a depth of insight that I, who thought I did, did not have before reading it.

I hope that it will help many of us, who in the past have been seen as on the opposite side, to become better advocates for all our 'special' children. I feel it will be invaluable as a resource for both teaching and learning. I particularly enjoyed the mixture of prose and poetry making the book easier to read. Within the prose some word pictures will stay with me. John Smith in writing of his son David gives the 'textbook' description, that 'one of the features of Down's syndrome is the stubby hand, with shorter than normal fingers'. John writes 'the diminutive hand whose fingers appear like the point of a star'. I shall never examine the hand of a child with Down's syndrome again without thinking of that star.

Gillian Upton Holmes writes 'my first and last wish for Hal is that those who support, teach and heal him should also love him'. I would not have included love as part of the requirement for working with children like Hal 'professionally'. But surely what this book is saying is that we should not only respond academically and scientifically but also emotionally. This writing has reinforced my feeling that we should not be afraid to show parents and children that although we do not have all the answers, we do share their love and delight in these special children.

Many parents reading this book will be at the beginning of their journey towards a lifestyle very different from any they had ever imagined. I feel that through its pages they will learn that they are not alone and gain some of the strength that is reflected in *Altered Images.*

Mary Jones

Mary Jones is a parent, consultant community paediatrician, adviser to Ryedale Special Families, gardener, and photographer and sometimes she tries a little poetry. She is Editor of BACCH News, the quarterly newsletter of the British Association for Community Child Health.

Making This Book

How it all started

Gillian Upton Holmes and I got to know each other in 1999 at an adult education class, Writing Your Life Story, that I taught. She brought tremendous intelligence and passion to all her writing, but especially to accounts of raising her son, Hal. I was impressed by the ways in which she challenged the medical and welfare discourses of disability to recognise parents as equivalent holders of expert knowledge. And I was in awe of her ability to do casual elegance and scarlet lipstick first thing in the morning. When she asked for my advice about her plan to bring together a group of parents of disabled children to write about and publish their experiences I was intrigued and excited. We discussed who might be available to co-facilitate sessions and as we did so I realised the only person I really wanted to recommend was myself, and so I did. Gillian's emphasis on lived experience as a check and balance to professional knowledge resonated with my practice of community writing and publishing. Although I was aware at the outset how little I knew about disability I was inspired by the observation of historian and one-time extramural lecturer Edward Thompson that it is the nature of adult educators to learn from as well as teach their students. This has never been truer for me than in the making of this book.

What was different about *Altered Images*?

The project Gillian outlined to me would break new ground by telling a story about parenting disabled children that was collective and complex. Just like the experience itself, the story would be open-ended and full of contradictions. Not only would it be rooted in experiences that were sometimes joyful and hopeful and sometimes desperate and grim, but it would also explain the fluid inter-connectedness of these states. The project would try to capture the variety of individual experience in order to make more complex the existing literature of disability, whether this took the form of individual testimony or official policy and training documents. By being truthful and unsentimental about the highs and the lows of learning to live with a disabled child *Altered Images* would not only offer comfort and advice from the inside but it would, to borrow a phrase from the Quakers, speak truth to power. What we mean by this is that *Altered Images* challenges official accounts of disability which, although they depend upon the experience of disabled people and their carers, do not enable them to participate in analysing and interpreting that experience. These official accounts not only have the power to tell disabled people and their carers what their lives mean but, because they determine financial and practical resources which have significant impact upon their lives, they are also able to impose their meanings in very direct ways.

While we were discussing and writing *Altered Images* people often referred to it as the book they wished they had been able to read. It is a kind of atlas of the new, parallel, universe that parents of disabled children enter and become citizens of. As people who had been there long enough for the shock to wear off, and for some of its ways to become familiar, the authors wanted to share their maps with those venturing into this strange world for the first time.

Who is *Altered Images* for?

Thinking about the readers of *Altered Images* as parents of newborn or newly diagnosed disabled children became an important touchstone for the group. But they were not the only intended audience. *Altered Images* was also the book that its authors wished others had read. Those others might include: doctors, grandparents, nurses, neighbours, social workers, in-laws, brothers and sisters, health visitors, friends, physiotherapists, parents, partners, work mates, neighbours, the other women in the maternity ward, people you went to school with, people who shopped in the same supermarkets, people who passed you in the street, anyone who stood and stared or looked away. It is a long list already, and incomplete. What it is, is a list of everyone who stands outside the experience of disability and puts up a barrier between their life and yours across which their pity, judgement, disgust, advice and opinion travels freely. This book was written for them, too.

How did we do it?

It took over three years to complete the book. Initially a series of fortnightly and then monthly meetings were held at which we talked about our plans for the group and began to generate ideas and writing. For the first year, the emphasis was on generating writing: actually finding ways to find the words for the experiences. Writing can be a very daunting activity for people, triggering as it so often does feelings of inadequacy linked to the writing they were required to do at school. But even people who enjoyed writing at school can quickly lose the habit and feel unsure about writing after a gap and even the most confident of writers can be intimidated by the prospect of writing for publication.

Quite a lot of the work I did was to provide people with frameworks to stimulate, gather and develop their writing. One of the most powerful myths about writing is that what we read as printed text is, or ought to be, the way writing arrives on the page. I helped to demystify the writing process that lies behind all finished pieces and helped the writers become confident in their judgements about when and how pieces were finished. Some of the group found writing easier than did others. As often happens in writing groups, one person's account would spark off memories and reactions from someone else and so the writing grew incrementally. We were fortunate enough to have funding that enabled us to go away for an overnight break at a retreat centre on two occasions. Although the logistical arrangements for this were daunting, the space and concentrated time to write free from domestic demands were fantastically important in creating a habit of writing, a body of work and, most importantly, the trust needed to write and share the writing.

It was electrifying when writing was read back and discussed in the group. Often, the group was elated by the power of the writing: its ideas, its style and its effect. Relief in sharing experience and understanding, at being able to laugh, cry and curse. Often, too, people were going back to very painful, sometimes humiliating, places in their lives. They remembered that they had simply had to get on with it at the time. They often felt guilty about what they had or hadn't done. They felt angry and they felt sad, for themselves and for each other. Listening was often as harrowing as writing and reading aloud the original accounts. Sometimes, just going back in time was overwhelming. Sometimes, and far more poignantly, what overwhelmed people was the realisation that things they had battled with in isolation, often to do with uncomfortable or shameful feelings, were familiar to the others. The powerful validation and release they experienced, through writing and being in the group, sometimes highlighted how much they had needed that support in the past, and how painfully lacking it had been.

Writing was undoubtedly a cathartic process, and one that was positive for everyone some of the time. It made *a* difference but it could not make *the* difference and it did not eradicate the everyday frictions and conflicts that always arise at some point in a group's life. If anything, because the writing group operated at such a deep emotional level, it sometimes made these dynamics all the more volatile. It is important for anyone reading this book who is thinking, "We could do that!" to know that they probably can, and almost certainly should. But it is also important to be aware that it is not a straightforward undertaking. However well planned and well organised the project, however skilled and sensitive the facilitator, however respectful the group members, tensions will arise. The group will fall out and some people, as happened to us, will become alienated and withdraw, leaving everyone hurt, disappointed and awkward with each other, for a while at any rate. Although we tried hard to do so, I don't think we could actually have prevented this from happening. It is part of the undertow of moving into the powerful territory of memory, hope and desire that any writing, but especially writing about a topic as complex and challenging as being and becoming parents of disabled children, involves.

We did not do this alone

There were many more people involved in making this book than its authors and editors. Some parents came to the discussions or helped with editing but did not contribute writing of their own and their contribution was just as valuable as were those of the parents who wrote the pieces. John Hancock provided invaluable support in the early stages of the project and assisted in accessing an initial grant from North Yorkshire Health Authority. Staff at RSF ensured funds were raised to complete the project and provided child-care, co-ordination, meeting space and photocopying during the project as well as agreeing to oversee the book's promotion and distribution. We found printers who understood the importance of the book and guided us gracefully and respectfully through the process of its production. Eileen Whittingham alchemised our scraps of handwriting into clean, typed copy. Family and friends lived with the disruption that writing and publishing inevitably brings in its wake and still encouraged us on our way.

Why It Matters

Making time for the searching reflection and writing that went into *Altered Images* was incredibly difficult for everyone; no one's lives as parents of disabled children could be put on hold while they worked on the book. It was difficult for me, too, sustaining a voluntary project through three of the most difficult years of my working life as the university I work for closed first the adult education centre and then the department of continuing education where I worked. I carried on because I knew this was going to be a good book, that there was nothing like it in the public domain and I had faith that we would finish it, eventually. My struggle to make time for the project brought home to me the real nature of the subject we were writing about. I did have the choice to walk away from the difficulties of completing and publishing the book but there was no walking away for the parents: they have to live its content 24 hours a day, every single day of their lives.

I know our efforts were worth it. The book you are about to read contains very different types of writing. This is deliberate and important. Disability is not a unitary experience, and nor are the families and communities where it is lived out. *Altered Images* contains autobiographical accounts, diary extracts, polemic and poetry. These different types of writing are each presented differently in the book, which talks about the kaleidoscope of emotions that parents of disabled children have to learn to live with and explores some of the rites of passage that await them. These include diagnosis, dealing with the professionals, making decisions about schooling, the consequences for family life, dealing with grief, and the struggle to understand their own and other people's attitudes to disability.

Altered Images changed how I think about and act towards disabled children and their parents, and I would like it to do the same for you, too. This is one example of how it was for me. As we neared publication one of my oldest and closest friends became a grandmother for the second time, to her first granddaughter. Born prematurely, in a Special Care Baby Unit 25 miles from home, it was clear at the outset that Rosa was not doing well. Within 48 hours she had been transferred across two counties to the nearest Neo-Natal Intensive Care Unit where, later that week, a consultant from a third hospital diagnosed a very rare genetic disorder. Initially given hours to live, she survived weeks, and then months. Rosa died in August 2005, at home, in her mother's arms, aged seven and a half months. I like to think that I would have behaved as calmly and supportively to my friend, her daughter and granddaughter whether or not I had known the authors of this book and their stories. But I know that is wishful thinking.

Without *Altered Images* my ignorance and insensitivity or ineptness caused by my fear of saying or doing the wrong thing would have made me part of the problem. No doubt, too, that I would also actually have said or done the wrong thing. The book gave me the privileged opportunity to learn from, as well as learn about, the lives of the parents on whose experience and ideas it is based. The project not only taught me things I did not know about disability, for example that neither electric wheelchairs nor Motability vehicles are provided free of charge, but it also helped me to see the differences between *knowing about* disabled children and their parents and *knowing how to behave* towards and around them. Understanding this difference made it possible for me to acknowledge the reality of what was happening in my friend's family, to know the importance of walking the journey with her, in whatever way she needed me to, and to keep offering emotional and practical help. I hope *Altered Images* can do the same for you, whether you are the parents of a newly diagnosed disabled child, their friends, family, work colleagues or neighbours or one of the myriad professionals they will encounter.

Rebecca O'Rourke

On Becoming A Warrior Parent

Bellicose images surround us parents with disabled children. You would think we were a fearsome warlike tribe like the Ashanti. We 'fight' for our children, getting services, education and Disabled Living Allowance is a 'battle'. If we want something we have to 'campaign' for it. If we don't like the way things are being done we 'stick our heads above the parapet'.

Some people spent their university days on demos, supporting the miners' strike, never happier than when waving free banners supplied by the Socialist Workers on a march for some cause or other. But I was never an activist. At my college few strong opinions were expressed except about the precise moment when wearing a ra-ra skirt became an absolute no-no.

Confronted by a problem I prefer to have a gin rather than do anything. No warrior parent armour for me thank you very much.

It was not until Hal was born that I was pitched into an arena where action was necessary, like it or not. I was forced to put on my armour and learn to fight for my child. I remember being in an almost permanent state of fury during the early years of Hal's diagnosis. I was particularly angry every time I was invited to attend a meeting or express my views on a questionnaire. It was all so boring, so solemn, so worthy. I'm no busybody. I have no interest in evangelising my neighbours into a happier, healthier way of life. Having a gin, as I may have said before, is preferable.

I Joined Up

But in the end I felt compelled to get involved. For once it was obvious that something needed to be done, and that I might even have something to contribute. That feeling helped overcome my self-doubt, and my laziness. The war effort needs YOU .... I joined up. I joined everything – local steering groups, national campaigns. Before long I had been elected chair of several committees and invited to become a trustee of the Family Fund.

I developed a Victorian sense of duty. In my obsession and commitment to advancing the cause of disabled children, I identified with the Lady campaigners who made the British Empire great, and I wrote their slogans on post-it notes. Momentarily I was dizzy with power and delusions of grandeur: internet personality tests gave me a profile somewhere between Margaret Thatcher and Saddam Hussein. But seriously ... my participation in this new world was both enjoyable and useful. It was reassuring to learn that my views born of direct experience were recognised and valued by independent experts, and supported by extensive research in the study of disabled children. It was enormously helpful to listen and talk to people with formidable intellectual gifts and national reputation, and have the chance to refine and distil my own ideas about education, health and social opportunities for Hal. I had always had the highest expectations for him. I was relieved to know that powerful and influential individuals were labouring to make these real.

I began to learn more about the unknown territory Hal and I had entered. I met consultants, health and education professionals outside an immediate personal context, and talking about the inherent and intractable obstacles in the system was reassuring and less stressful than talking specifically about Hal. The warrior hackles were momentarily smoothed.

Token Parent?

I was in the process of becoming a kind of hybrid creature – a professional parent of a disabled child. This felt safer than the experience of early months and years when ignorance and fear meant that I was tensed against every new development. There are parents who go to war on behalf of their own children and those who become radicalised and so start to campaign in a more general way. But it is dangerously easy to be drawn into the world of disability professionalism. New transparency and openness diktats mean that every statutory and voluntary organisation which provides anything at all for children with disabilities is eager to ensure that parents are represented on every last committee, sub-committee and sub-committee working group. I often felt like the token parent. You could, I promise you, fill your life with attending meetings.

Involving parents may also be exploitative and cruel. It is heartbreaking to watch vulnerable and anxious parents called out to hear the announcement that a special school is to be closed or a respite facility lost due to a lack of money, change of policy or 'reallocation of local authority resources'. Parents are called along, it is claimed, so that their voices can be heard, but I think it is often no more than a cynical exercise by service managers. I have sometimes felt we parents are being set up, pawns in a competitive funding game. It's as if they are saying, "Look at them crying! Now give us the money." This politics of pity and the denial of dignity it involves leads directly to angry and alienated families, parents unable to trust the very agencies who ought to be helping them to cope cheerfully with their challenges. Furious warrior parents.

It is important not to be taken in by the rhetoric of war. Almost invariably when I meet the parent of a newly diagnosed child, she will be bristling with the panoply of war, a latter day Boadicea, knives flashing at her chariot wheels, bearing down upon a cowering and bewildered bunch of NHS staff and social workers. She is a terrifying sight, and in her I see myself.

All Parents Become Warrior Parents

On the other hand, it is important not to lose the fire which lights up the true warrior parent. Living day by day with a disabled person, your child, and witnessing at first hand the contrast between your love and hope for him, and the world's flaccid indifference, radicalises you. Anger, outrage and the need to put it right are inevitable consequences of your experience. I think this is why all parents become warrior parents. Not willingly or because that is our disposition, but because the system is set up for conflict. It shouldn't be. But while it is, every time a parent questions a decision or asks for a better service she is forced to engage in battle

The fight can be very lonely. In the early days, before I got to know other parents and all those who understand the challenges we face, I felt isolated. I had a fragile sense of self worth and low confidence, I felt out of joint, not one of the crowd, a problem, and I hated the feeling. Ours is an age which regards conflict and disagreement with exaggerated distaste so it is often difficult to be cast in the role of a warrior parent. It is so important in the culture of positive thinking not to be construed as criticising anyone. The various professionals and organisations with whom we are forced into contact, and sometimes conflict, have their early warning systems, surface to air missiles and escape bunkers ready before we have even received our call-up papers.

The weapons that may be used against a warrior parent are many. There are those who say they "admire your passion", but we need to remember that our enthusiastic suggestions for change are being heard in the context of the expert world which values coolness and detachment. A parent invited onto a committee may soon be seen as a loose cannon, whose guns must be spiked. There are essays, whole books even, which pathologise the involvement of parents in campaign groups and support networks as "suppressed grief" or "denial". There are even people out there waiting to put you down for your articulacy and determination on your child's behalf. Smoothly (almost as if they had practised it) they will tell you that of course you are middle-class and articulate, but not all parents are, and that squeaking doors get the most oil, that by asking for what seems fair to you, that you are in fact being unfair to those who are not asking at all. I think this is an unscrupulous argument, playing off one family against another, need against need. Criteria and precise allocation of budgets meanwhile remain a closely guarded secret. The professionals who use these tactics may not intend to erode or depress parents by talking in this way, but the effect is the same.

There is a certain conversation I often have with such parents, the kind who might reasonably be described as activists – well-informed, motivated people who turn up at national conferences. They will tell a story about unjust treatment, shoddy service or shocking incompetence and then say, "If they could do this to *me* then what is happening to everyone else?"

Dry Powder and Clear Heads

The truth is that we are a numerically small and politically insignificant group. I suspect that is why parents often resort to melodramatic outbursts in the local press when fobbed off once too often. Though I have sympathy with the sense of frustration, which may be slaked by 'going public', I think we need to be cleverer than this: we must demonstrate clearly that we are capable of rational discussion. We must keep our powder dry and our heads clear. We are most powerful when our words have a force derived from hard experience and long meditation. Another danger is that we invoke the tragedy model of disability: when we do this the best we can hope for is pity. And pity, far from helping the observer to engage with our feelings, distances him and allows him to turn – sadly – away. I think it is dangerous to encourage anyone, and especially those in positions of power, to see us in this way. Rather we should seek to persuade, educate and cheerfully convince everyone we meet.

This requires self-control – difficult when we feel so passionately about the issues. But we cannot browbeat others into understanding our position. Nor should we resort to emotional blackmail, or self-indulgent displays of anguish. The short-term relief we may gain will lead to long term losses. How many meetings with parents have been shelved because 'We don't want to risk upsetting them', and thereby how many opportunities to improve circumstances for ourselves, our children and countless others? Professionals have a right to protect themselves from personal attack and emotional outbursts which set back the process of working towards change. It is crucial that we remember this and if forced to engage in battle that we exercise restraint.

When I was new to this arena, I remember hearing another parent talk about the importance of being courteous and polite. As someone who tends to fly off the handle too easily, I resolved to change and hard though it has been, I have tried to establish equal, reasonable and productive relations with the people who work with my son. They have after all chosen to make their life's work in an area which I know can be frustrating, difficult and unrecognised. In the main they are my allies not my enemies. I began to avoid the people who made me feel worse not better (what one writer describes as the 'nocebo' effect) and I developed a nose for the people who emphasised what we can do to make positive changes.

One of our great strengths as parents is our independence. Not getting our wages from the Local Education Authority or the National Health Service means that if we spot weaknesses in the system we have the freedom to say so. Many professionals, the positive people, understand this and give us covert encouragement and support because we can help to bring about changes they have long wanted to see. But it is important that we are not getting our core support from the same people whom we may need to be critical of. This is why I am dubious about many so-called support groups set up within schools, child development centres and so on. Such groups often serve to contain and defuse our concerns, rather than encouraging parents to challenge, confront and bring about change. And it is doubly important that family support groups, which are frequently set up by parents seeking to create a voice for families, do not get drawn in to service provision at the expense of their representative role.

Expert Parents?

I've found that just keeping going can be very hard. One of the roles of a truly supportive group is to be an Ops Room to which we can return having tackled difficult professionals, either on behalf of our own child or as a 'representative' of other parents. A good support group (which might be made up of only one or two people) will provide a safe atmosphere of shared experience, understanding and sympathy, not to mention humour. Without such support, I for one would have found it difficult to maintain *sang froid*, keep my sanity and live to fight another day. Parents sometimes become cynical and therefore ineffective when their child has been in the system too long. Cynicism can set in when the optimism of ignorance is tempered by the disappointment of a little knowledge. Good support helps us to move from stage to stage with confidence, valuing the insight which even negative experience brings.

Politicians and disability professionals are now talking about 'expert parents', but I've got a problem with the word expert. The modern sense of 'expert' implies theoretical knowledge and skill in analysing objective evidence. Parents' expertise comes from direct experience, and in that sense it is closer to the Latin root of the word *experior* – to experience, to endure. But I prefer the word amateur. I want to be an amateur with its roots in the Latin word *amare* to love.

In the end, you see, I believe that love is more powerful than war. My first and last wish for Hal is that those who support, teach and heal him should also love him. That is what we warriors are really fighting for and the one thing we are uniquely qualified to understand. Parents after all are people who do it for love.

Gillian Upton Holmes

Imagine

Imagine living in a world where people are valued
for being whoever they are.
Where intellect is not valued over a beautiful soul
Where doing is not encouraged over being
Where dreams are valued for the quality of their dreaming
Where the awareness of judgement, suspicion and mistrust
have run their course and been discarded
in the name of love
Where all are encouraged to dream dreams, reach potential,
fly and soar above, below, around and beyond. Imagine.

A Mum

1 A Very Bleak Diagnosis

Precious

You were tiny, minute, but just the most beautiful baby I ever laid eyes on. I was your mummy and I could see past the tubes, past the machines, past the oscillating ventilator that was making your whole body vibrate.

To me, you were here – you had been for five hours now and I had to believe my gut feeling. The gut feeling that said, "Everything would be ok", despite what *they* were telling me. It was now 8pm.

"Do you want me to call the Chaplain?" the nurse said to me.

"Do I need to call the Chaplain?" I replied.

"I think you should," said the nurse.

I looked at her and saw pity in her eyes. "No," I wanted to scream. "No, this wasn't necessary. No, it shouldn't be like this. Where are the smiles, the congratulations, the cards, flowers, balloons and teddies … ." But it was like this and, as realisation set in, I needed the Chaplain. I needed the comfort that perhaps, just perhaps, we could change that pity in her eyes to joy!

So we stood late that evening and joined hands around your bed, fitting in around the machines and drips and behind the screen that had now been erected around your bed. I remember feeling calm, but being aware that other than myself, your Grandma and the Chaplain, everyone else still held that pity in their eyes. It stayed in the eyes of people for weeks. But slowly it changed. You could see their faces saying "Perhaps, just perhaps!" But on the whole, nobody dared to hope too much, and at times I admit I found myself joining in.

Your lung would collapse. Your toes would turn black, causing the Duty Registrar to break into a sweat, trying desperately to save them from dropping off. The list went on and on. Sometimes it all became too much. I resisted the urge to touch you or hold you, because after all if *they* were going to be right then it would be easier if I didn't get too close, wouldn't it? Each night we had to drive home, had to leave you with people who sometimes seemed to have taken my role. We would drive through the chaos of the East End, down the even more chaotic motorways, often in silence or tears, and always staring at my mobile, praying it wouldn't ring. Praying you *would* get through the night. You just had to.

After seven weeks and several cancellations you were finally getting your transfer out of N.I.C.U (neonatal intensive care unit) to S.C.B.U. (special care baby unit). A promotion! And an apology – from a Doctor. The man who had told me, the day before you were born, that his advice was to "Leave him in there and let him go". He had been with you for seven weeks now and he knew he'd been wrong. As everyone around us began to relax, for us the fear really took a tight grip. We were nearing the Next Level. This level involved bringing you home, along with the latest addition to our family – your tubes. The oxygen points were wired around our home in order for you to leave hospital. But that meant it was Us vs. Your Lungs. No panic button, No Senior House Officers or Registrars. Just Mummy, Daddy and a video on step-by-step resuscitation.

Heidi Ridgewell

You Were So Tiny

You came into the world at 14.49 pm. Born by Caesarean Section, you weighed 2lb 14oz. Daddy and I saw you briefly before you were whisked away to an awaiting array of Doctors and Nurses. You are a very poorly little boy. You are three months premature and have a very big cyst on your lung. This has made your heart weak. They have taken you away from us to begin trying to make you better.

Notes

I have spoken to parents briefly this am and painted a very bleak prognosis with the possibility of their baby not surviving resuscitation at birth, but there seems little doubt that delivery was necessary. They now understand that the mass is compromising the lungs and cardiac status and I have explained that this resolution can only be achieved by surgery.

They are fully aware of the severity of his current state.

At 8pm the Chaplain visits. We have you blessed and pray to God that you will still be here tomorrow.

17 January 1999

You are in the Neonatal ICU at The Royal London Hospital. Although extremely poorly, you are alive, something nobody expected. Daddy and I just sit and stare at you. It hasn't all sunk in yet. It has been decided that you will go to Great Ormond St., for an operation to remove the bad part of your lung and put your heart back in the right place. We are terrified, but know that we have no choice but to give our consent. So we'll just pray to God that you are ok!

Notes

He had right middle lobectomy at 36hrs of age. The post-operative period was complicated by hypothermia with a temp of 29 degrees on return from theatre. Charlie lost his bodily blood twice over, causing anaemia, which was corrected pre-operatively. His pupils were large and non-reactive.

18 January 1999

After an extremely long and restless night, we begin to relax as you arrive back at The Royal. You've fought so very hard. I don't think we'll ever be able to tell you how very proud of you we are.

19 January 1999

Am. Today has been a good day. We can seé such an improvement in you. You've lost a lot more fluid, particularly from your face, which means we can see your little features.

Nannie and Grandad and Grandma have been here today and they adore you. Then you opened your eyes; just before they left.

P.M. It seems that you opened your eyes, not because of improvement as we thought but because you were in pain. You began to thrash about. Your morphine has been increased and at last they have been able to settle you.

My precious baby. I cannot begin to tell you how much we want to take you away from all of this. The phrase 'my heart is breaking' has become real for Daddy and I. A path is appearing. The path the three of us are beginning to take; and there isn't anything either of us wouldn't do, in order to take a diversion away from this.

We love you, Night, night Sweetheart.

20 January 1999

You are amazing Charlie. You have started trying to make breaths on your own. We are so happy. During today, you have improved so much.

Your Daddy can't stop touching you, he changes your enormous nappy, cleans your eyes and mouth with a cotton bud. Mummy? Well, Mummy's a little more nervous. You are so tiny and look so fragile that I find it all very scary. Your skin is so thin that when the Doctors hold a torch over your chest, they can see your heart beating! One day, you'll think that is really cool but right now it scares me.

We've named you Action Man, not only because they are the only clothes that would fit you right now, but because you are such a little fighter.

21 January 1999

Today has been a very busy day for you and in your own way quite traumatic. You've a little jaundice so you are underneath two bright lights with your hat pulled over your eyes and that is how you've remained all day. Your right arm and left leg have been elevated to try and help along the healing process of your burns. During the night we had a very close call with your tiny toes which all went black but by this morning, although a little dusky, they are pink again.

It seems every obstacle thrown at you, you leap! Grandma and Nannie came to visit today and were delighted to see the change in you. You won't see Grandma for two weeks now but her love is still around you constantly. Your Auntie Sarah and Uncle David sent the most beautiful flowers for daddy and me: the bouquet is bigger than you.

This afternoon Dr Paul removed your chest drain. Again it was your daddy who stayed with you during the procedure. Everything looks fine, we'll just await an x-ray tonight. You look more relaxed, even though you are more covered in bandages and tubes. Mummy and daddy cried buckets tonight. We have to go home tomorrow and start travelling during the week and weekends. It is so hard to have to leave you here but the decision is not in our hands. We have faith in your team of Doctors and Nurses and I know that God will watch over you. We love you deeply and our hearts are aching already but we must go home to prepare it for you. Night, night sweetheart.

11.00pm

I've just held you in my arms for the very first time. It was the most amazing feeling I have ever had. You are now settled into a proper incubator and look like you're cosy, so I think you'll sleep easier. God Bless xxxxx

Notes

Called out for blue feet L recovered 4th toe R foot cyanosed.

Peripheral pulses not felt in upper limbs

Harsh breath sounds

22 January 1999

You look like an angel that has slept blissfully. Daddy and mummy changed your nappy again. You are stretching your legs and arms amazingly well. An ultrasound has shown that your kidneys are fine, as is your heart. So today has been a good day for you. Tonight we are home and missing you like crazy but we are preparing the house for you. We go to sleep still feeling the touch of your skin and the grip of your fingers and toes.

23 January 1999

"Happy birthday". Today you are one week old. Something nobody dared to hope would happen. Daddy phoned the ward first thing. You've taken a step back overnight. Your chest drain must go back in and so you are not as stable as we'd like. It is making our first day away from you even harder. It also made it very difficult for Grandma to go home. All we can do is keep the phone-line to God busy!

Notes

Charlie having been well overnight became unwell this am. Half an hour after which he began losing blood. Treatment didn't result in any significant improvement in baby as he became more pale and mottled. Morphine dose upped, chest x-ray done, clotting sent and in view of pallor packed cells ordered.

Chest x-ray showed recurrence of pneumathorax, had chest drain re-inserted under sterile conditions.

24 January 1999

Today Auntie Tracy has met you. You gripped her little finger with your hand, which was a very special moment. You are very poorly and stressed but we've sat with you today and watched you sleeping. This afternoon you had a little operation to put a new line into you. You've handled the procedure very well and you are peaceful, so we left you to sleep. God Bless you Angel xxxxx

25 January 1999

Well done darling! You've been a good boy today. Tonight you had a chest x-ray which showed that your lung is ok. Your blood pressure is up and down but with everything you've been through it isn't surprising. We are missing you all the time. So we end tonight hoping that you are back on track for a speedy recovery, then we can transfer you to Colchester and we can spend every day with you.

26 January 1999

You continue to amaze us Charlie. On arrival today, we were both amazed by how fantastic you look. You are constantly taking breaths and moving around. You gripped our fingers with all the strength and determination you've proved to have so much of during the last 10 days. You look so beautiful and so peaceful compared to previous days. Daddy is so relaxed that tonight he "sleeps like a baby". Mummy is on a high and can't sleep! So I lie in bed and thank God for keeping watch over you.

27 January 1999

Today you did your first poo!!! As you are reading this now, you'll think it odd that this is such a big deal. But trust me, it is a wonderful sign for us and the Doctors that everything is in working order. So we are ecstatic.

28 January 1999

Today your chest drain came out for a second time and we hope to God that it is for the last time. You have also had your first milk, which we know will do you the world of good. You are comfortable and well. You are totally amazing.

29 January 1999

So far, so good. The chest drain has stayed out and the nurse has just phoned to say that you are laid on your tummy for the first time and looking blissfully comfortable. We drove down to see you this afternoon. You look so much better and even managed to open your eyes and grip our fingers. You have begun to have milk and Daddy fed you your 7pm feed through your tube. It seems to get harder to leave you each time.

30 January 1999

Just phoned the hospital. You are now on 1 ml of milk per hour. Brilliant. You are trying all the time to take your own breaths, although at the moment they want you to rest but you have your own ideas. We'll see you tomorrow, so sleep well and be good.

31 January 1999

We came to see you today with Nannie and Grandad. On the whole we had a good day. You look very well but you got a little stressed and so you had to have a little sedation. Your milk has been increased and so now you have 1.5ml per hour. You are taking it well and doing lots of poo-poos. Before we left tonight you had your nappy changed and whilst the nurse was doing it, you cried. There was no noise because you are on a ventilator, but the facial expression was all there – yet another sign that you are progressing.

Heidi Ridgewell

My Sunshine

I was drained by the year; the last drops of being had been spent with David's admission into hospital with pneumonia. The fight had gone. I could do no more than exist – eat, sleep, work without plan, drive unthinking – the joy was gone. Silence beckoned. David had no more smiles – just whimpers of pain when being fed. He wanted food, but could not cope with the agony of swallowing. He wanted water to quench his thirst, but could only take an insufficient drop at a time, from the edge of a spoon. All this was Nature's painful joke. And then he slept … and slept … David was eight months old. He had spent half his brief life in hospital wards, with an oxygen tube scarring his nostrils and a pulsating SATs monitor agonising his tiny foot. And now he was back … . in the hospital where he was born. The most painful blow of all, after the foolish return to normal life over the previous four months. But this is how it had all started …

Thursday

"Is there a Dr. Smith here, please?" The voice was Limerick, as was the place and the time.

"There's a phone call for you, from your wife."

How? … She knew I was working in Ireland but how has she traced me here, this morning? Why? Why is she sobbing? There's something wrong with the baby … what? scan? … growth on back of head? … sobbing …

'I'll be back tonight … I'll be back tonight.' Numb. Nothing. Must finish lecture … Everything on hold … Finish lecture …

Numbness melts to a deep silence in the airport lounge … accepting the unacceptable … a deformed and suffering baby, struggling for life in the dark places. An unbelievable joke from a believable God? Why? – The silence of why?

The rest of the day was nothing. (Now, with the distance of time, I see that I received kindness from beautiful souls, who comforted and supported; then, it seemed nothing.) Dark travel to my destination, more sobbing and the black night of a universal pain enveloping the world, a midnight ride back to our home.

We hug before we leave for Scan 2; the horror of losing our unborn gnaws, not the horror of deformity, but the horror of the decision demanded of us to consider ending it all now … the hopelessness of the invitation … and the perpetual night of having agreed. But we still hug … the three of us, one unborn – almost unbeing, and we pray together for release … and comfort comes – 'though you pass through the deep waters, you will not be overwhelmed' … and I begin to weep my first tear of relief, my first tear of comfort, my first tear of hope.

Friday

Scan 2 … Mention of Down's and heart problems. The offer of tests. And we dithered, refused, not wanting the burden of the decision, then accepting, trusting the eminent physician, but wary that we might cause damage. But his skill was sufficient, his care was gentle although he gave us the agony of waiting ... waiting ... waiting … waiting … The results lumbered on. At home we waited, dazed and silent, but together, as one, though three … still three! We would not let the unknown go – if he was to go he would have to choose not us. We would protect him from harm, if he would fight for being. The weekend passed – neither sluggishly nor fleetingly – but at surprisingly normal pace. The fears were submerged, normality strangely reigned. We told no one and waited for Monday for the fear to surface.

Monday

The raw terror of unknowing tore at us. We rang the hospital early, very early, but were ordered to wait until the designated hour. The demons of terror rushed in. We begged in prayer, we bargained with God, we offered our very sanity for release. Our minds cracked, but a strange peace came in each other's arms; we slumbered entwined in a chair. The three of us, protecting each other from the demons; it was they who fled from us in terror. One o'clock came gently.

"The tests were positive, I am afraid; the baby has Down's. It is in every cell, not Mosaic." *(Mosaic Down's is a less severe form of Down's affecting 3 per cent of children with the syndrome; they have a mixture of normal cells and those containing the extra number 21 chromosome and are less affected physically and mentally.)*

Sue began to groan from the depth of her being; the future beckoned – a different, unknown and unpredictable future. Her groan let the vision go. It was the first letting go of an ideal that would not now be; our agony was for our gullibility in dreaming, our inability to guide the future by past thought. Her groan was of childbirth and child-death, the parched, tearless cry of destruction, which pierced my own soul.

"Stop, Susan, you are breaking my heart!"

And her love for me silenced her agony.

The phone was still there, unfeeling; the doctor was there with compassion:

"Is that Susan? ... Do you want someone to come to help?"

But the comfort was salve to a wound that had started to heal. She regained a teary composure.

"Ask him if it is a boy or girl."

"A boy." The coffin of our vision baby (a girl) now slammed shut.

"It is a boy!" ... The present tense resounded. It was not future, not 'never' tense.

"It *is* a boy!"

He went on, somewhat dispassionately now:

"You will have to talk. We will respect any decision you make. He does have a severe heart complaint. We will arrange a further scan for you. I am so sorry."

The conversation ended. I thanked him and the phone was put to rest again. We hugged in silence, lost now in the depth of ourselves, not thinking of ourselves as three, not even as two, but as nothing. We would ponder on an unformed heart chamber and wait again.

We had a new road, a new future; yet so much was the same road. We ate the same food, went for the same walks in the countryside, and did the same work. Our friends were the same, our family the same, mother-in-law the same; not devastated, but sympathetic as always, respecting our pain. We slept and woke as normal, even joked as normal, with a new subject now as we laughed at Down's with our unborn son. Our unborn had a sense of humour and helped to heal us, helped us to love and accept him. The news warned of genetically modified tomatoes, and we had a genetically modified son!

David has now gone! His love remains with us, his smile remains in our memories and hearts. His joy-smile first thing in the morning to say, 'Greetings, Daddy, I love you and life is such fun!' His joy-smile at my gurning, at my hand clap to pick him up. How he helped at nappy changes by clutching his ankles. How he adored tapping cupboard handles. There are smiles still with me. The sunshine he gave to all. My son: thank you for loving us. Will we skip with you again? Will we dance, laugh, blow your raspberries, be joyful deeper than smiles? Will we run and chase and see your transcendence, your awe of the dancing leaf, of the speck of a soaring bird, your seraphic radiance?

Everything was new for him – and he helped us to see the new. The loss is absolute and uncompromising but it is old, past, gone. The new still beckons.

And David would smile ...

Is smiling ...

John Smith

A dozen things they don't warn you about when your baby is born with special needs

1. You are expected to know that "Skuboo", surely a cartoon character, is actually SCBU and stands for Special Care Baby Unit.
2. BO is bowels opened and PU is passed urine.
3. How hard it is to be in a maternity ward without a baby beside your bed.
4. How intimately you will become acquainted with a breast pump and how you will start making surreptitious comparisons with other mums on Special Care. How much have they produced, how many of their storage bottles in the freezer?
5. How quickly your world will shrink, to your baby, your room and the Special Care Baby Unit.
6. How after just nine days you will be driven home for the night by your husband and be gazing in wonder out of the car window. "Oh yes, there's the Spar shop and the post box – it's just as I remember." As if you're taking a sentimental journey back in time to a former life, a former place you once lived.
7. How terrified you will be after three months at the thought of coming home; of being a grown up responsible person again, of running a house, paying bills, cooking meals, maintaining a relationship.
8. How much you will come to depend on the routine of the institution – regular mealtimes, the sponge and custardness comfort of hospital food.
9. How awkward it feels to be an exhibit for the student doctors to gawp at on their rounds. ("And here is a fine example of a typical distraught mother of a disabled baby. Notice how she is not dressed yet and has not got her emotions in check.")
10. That every gram your baby gains or loses will really, really matter. That you'll rush to the 'phone to tell mum the splendid news that he's put on 480g, only to be utterly devastated later to discover it's just fluid and not "proper" weight

11. That you will provide extra interest and entertainment on a Sunday afternoon for all the extra friends and relatives that come to visit the other mums and their babies. Once their initial flurry of interest and excitement is over, eyes begin to wander to the next cot, eyes meet yours, polite enquiries are made and they come over uninvited to stare and chat and coo. You put on the act for their benefit but feel like a freak show. It gets unreal when you're explaining which bit of the breast pump goes where to the elderly man fascinated by all the machinery.
12. How well you will get to know the machinery. That soon you will be casually flicking switches off and resetting alarms to the horror and fascination of your visitors. You will know which beeps, dings or chimes are important, and which are not.

Sue Smith

A Journey

Sharing with other mothers in the Writing Group has allowed me somehow to lift a lid and peek inside myself. Looking into the eyes of another mum opening up, bravely allowing me to see her pain in the raw, somehow allowed me to let go. In that moment, I felt free to just be me and express myself.

I have been aware for as long as I can remember that, when my emotions become overwhelming, I switch into an autopilot setting and function on a mechanical level. What has been a revelation to me is the fact that my autopilot setting has a life of its own, and I am squashed somewhere below it. Seeing these words written down is very uncomfortable for me.

The year 1985. Status: separated with two almost grown up children. I lived, loved, experienced, learnt with them, from them and through them. I owe them all so much. Now the time had come for me to think a little about my future, realise my dreams, my desires. Divorce on the horizon, the hard uphill jog of motherhood now to the side of me, time for lateral thinking. New doors were opening, new career, time for me, the world was my oyster.

Pregnant. I watched all the new doors slamming shut. The doctor offered abortion, for a moment a glimmer of light. Weighing up freedom versus guilt. I slammed the door shut myself.

Life soon took control of all decisions. Bleeding started at a trickle. I was swept along with the torrent of bed rest on top of bed rest and then more bed rest. The trickle was gushing by 23 weeks gestation. Even sadder, the doctors felt forced to give up on the welfare of the baby and I became their only priority. Labour was induced and I just lay pushing away my greatest fear, the moment of birth. I didn't want to be alone, but I was, no matter how many people surrounded me. The depth of my fear about the pain that my child might suffer compared only with the fear of my imagined loss. That feeling of dread has never left me, even though she was born alive with enough spirit to, at least, survive. I shall never forget the sound of the soulful gasp she made as they swept her away to the neo-natal ward on the top floor of the building.

There lay my tiny piece of stardust, with enough spirit to fill a universe, surrounded by a fish bowl, bleeping computers and yards of tubing. I hardly dare touch her tinyness after I had hobbled two floors to reach her. The doctor said to see if she survived twelve hours, then twenty-four, then thirty-six. But even then, there were still a lot of sharks in the water. She was ventilated for four long weeks. I was torn by the needs of my children at home and by those of my newborn baby. Emotions squashed, and with my gear firmly set on autopilot, I began the long, uphill trudge. Four long months I journeyed from home to hospital feeding my baby, returning home to feed my other children lunch returning to hospital to feed baby, return home to make their tea, return to hospital in the evening to feed baby, then finally returning home exhausted to flop into bed.

All the time baby was moving up the line of cots from constant care to hourly care, moving from her 1lb 14oz birth weight ounce by ounce, tube by tube, away from the machines and constant clicks, to a quieter, more normal existence.

I remember one day she had been moved to another space in the line of sleeping cots and I didn't know where she was, I didn't know which baby was mine. Fear and disorientation set in, then panic. I couldn't ask anyone which baby was mine, I was supposed to be a mother, I was supposed to instinctively know. I ran out, I ran away and asked my other daughter to find her sister. She instinctively knew where to look. Panic over, but I felt so incompetent, and I wanted to hide it. I didn't want anyone to see me.

I was desperately waiting to hear that my baby had gained enough weight to be allowed home. The magic figure of 5lbs took four long, hard, months and we had many traumatic moments when she crashed. Too many moments like that.

She needed an apnoea monitor to check her breathing before we could bring her home and, of course, lots of follow-up appointments, but I thought the worst was behind us and life would settle back down into normality. That person, the proud mother, taking her baby home after a four month long struggle is unrecognisable to me now. She thought the long hard struggle was behind her. She didn't know it was just beginning. She had a very fixed viewpoint of life, and thought she was going back into her old comfortably controlled world of motherhood. She had already unconsciously planned and chartered out the life of protective love; first steps into the garden, experiencing, exploring, reaching out for fun, excitement, pictured in a school uniform, ballet, swimming lessons, terrible teens, hard, but all part of the colourful tapestry of life. She had yet to see the edges of the extremes, but all was about to be unveiled, revealed and then torn to shreds.

For the moment, life settled down into taking time to enjoy my new larger family. Normal household chores resumed their satisfying routine: everything neat, clean, tidy and loved. Hospital appointments were kept religiously; the doctors were very pleased with her progress. My halo was polished and sat righteously on my head during every promptly kept visit, but with every visit, every appointment, I buried the doubt. It was squashed into that place of shared denial, between the hospital and me.

I remember a kind aunt who found the courage to touch this fearful place. "Just like a rag doll", she quietly whispered. Those words were quickly banished to that deep dark place inside. Visits to 'mothers and toddlers' were quickly terminated after my little baby lay alone, motionless in a buggy, as all the other active babies rolled, bounced, and tottered with delight between and around chattering, giggling, proud delighted mums. I sat quietly, motionless, at a distance.

Time stood still. I carried, loved, cared for my rag doll, as the weeks passed into months, avoiding contact with other children, filtering out comments I didn't want to hear, clinging to the doctor's words that developmental delay among prems was normal and that she might catch up. I drew denial round me like a warm comforting blanket, wrapping it round and round.

A lifetime has passed; my baby has grown and developed. Not as I wanted, not as I had planned. The future was not as I had anticipated. I spent the ensuing years striving for normality but I had to learn that normality is elusive.

Armed with the diagnosis cerebral palsy I became a woman with a mission. I digested all the books, contacted umpteen organisations, went to a zillion meetings, travelled far and wide for help. I was unstoppable, often obsessional. I knew best. I wouldn't listen to professionals. Sometimes I was right (however, my heartfelt thanks goes out to each and every one of them, especially the ones, I threw out of my way in my quest for knowledge). Life for my child became repetitive, regimented, a daily routine of physio', eating, physio', outings, physio', and, exhausted, sleeping. In a good position, of course. She was going to swim, cycle, walk. It was my way of coping. She was going to be as 'normal' as possible. Our holidays consisted of abseiling, canoeing, archery, orienteering, horse riding and travelling along a zip wire.

I think you get the picture. This doesn't mean we didn't have some wonderful times. It wasn't what I was doing that was wrong, only the reason why. This is a critical account. I am being hard on myself, as usual, but not as hard as I was being on my daughter. She wasn't allowed to travel in a wheelchair, she rode on a special three wheeler bike. She swam with the old age pensioners before going to school on a morning. From the age of three, she travelled 50 miles 'out of county' every day to attend a school for children with cerebral palsy. A placement I had fought the Local Education Authority for tooth and nail. However, this was my first U-turn. She hated it. I fought just as hard to get her out. I forged a new path, for just as long as I could.

I remember when the horrendous surgery first began. Years of white plaster and wonderful nurses who gave me life saving cups of tea as my heart broke. Watching the clock tick for hours, waiting for my precious child to come out of theatre, and then spending days and nights surviving the fear, pain and anguish. I remember after one hip operation she was waiting in her hip spiker (her legs were splayed and set), waiting for the paramedics to transfer her into the ambulance to take us home, at last. They refused to take us on safety grounds; they couldn't get her to fit on the bed. I forget now how we made it home.

What am I trying to say? What do all of my ramblings mean? You can make of them what you will. I think I would say, at the time, I did my best, because in amongst all of it, in amongst all the anguish and heartache, there has been a lot of laughter, wrapped up in endless love. If I had my time again, I think I would tell my child she didn't need any external input to be perfect. She is and always has been 'perfect', just the way she is. But to realise this I had to let go of what I wanted, what I had planned and anticipated. I had to learn to love her for the beautiful, gentle person she was born to be. All these qualities she already possessed, without any input from me.

The only ingredient I can ever add to make life normal is love, which at times has appeared elusive, and for that I am truly sorry. No matter how far apart the extremes in life seem to be, love always finds a way of drawing them closer together till you find that perfect place in the middle called normal. I don't expect to always own it but, when it appears, I value it. My daughter doesn't need to see these words to know them. We learned them together.

A Mum

First Diagnosis

Hal was born at home on Tuesday 7 December 1993. My labour was miraculously short or so it seemed to me who had spent forty-two frustrating hours in labour with my first son T. From the first slight pangs to the delivery of a healthy baby boy took four hours. And he had been born at home! I sat up in bed drinking champagne and basked in the congratulations.

A Good Baby

Hal was a good baby, he was quiet, not a demanding and voracious feeder like his brother had been. He was happiest cradled snoozing in my arms. There seemed to be no reason for concern. He startled incredibly easily, his arms and legs shot into the air at the slightest sound – the Moro reflex common to all infants.

As he grew older, eight weeks, twelve weeks, an insidious niggling question began to form in my mind about his progress. At the same age T. had been a great bouncing mountain of a child. In his christening photo taken at two months he is sitting on my knee, squeezed with difficulty into the family christening dress. At five months he could pull himself to standing in his cot, by seven months he was wobbling along pushing a toddle truck. Surely my memory was not deceiving me?

Sleeping peacefully in his pram Hal seemed like a real baby compared with superbaby T. So I tried to lay my anxious thoughts to rest. But Hal was prone to a strange phenomenon, a kind of doubling up, drawing his knees to his stomach, then stiffening, staring. He was sleeping a lot. When he sat in his baby seat he always turned to the right. And he didn't smile.

Only Colic

A. and I took him to see our GP first. He reassured us: said it was only colic and suggested we try gripe water to relieve the spasms. We were relieved at his common sense advice. It was of course what we wanted to hear. But the nagging doubt remained. Hal was so floppy and listless. Alone with him, I begged him to straighten and pull to sitting again and again. I would hold his wrists and pull him to sit urging him "Come ON Hal", and again and again his head would loll back, and prayers unanswered, overcome by futility, I wept dry-eyed despair.

What does a graduate mother living in the middle of rural North Yorkshire do when confronted with a problem? She consults a book. I read everything I could lay my hands on, but this little extract struck a dreadful chord. Re-reading it now brings back the butterflies in the stomach, the tightness around the temples I felt then as I sat in my bedroom, on a darkening spring evening, and read:

Infantile spasm. Also known as 'salaam attacks' because child doubles up at waist in an attitude of prayer. Attacks last for up to 2 seconds and may come on twice or three times a day. Causes include brain damage at birth, lack of oxygen or sugar in blood going to brain, brain infection and metabolic diseases such as phenylketonuria; can also be an after effect of whooping cough vaccine. Unfortunately attacks can cause or aggravate brain damage.

The words had a horrible fascination, I must have read them a thousand times in the ensuing months. Was this what was wrong with Hal? It couldn't be. Not my beautiful child who seemed to have an almost otherworldly quality as he stared at me with a look of complete trust, nestled into the crook of my arm, and fell asleep. I fought the doubts, continued to hope, believed with a grim and determined faith that all would be well.

Almost Perfect

Hal was christened in a crypt chapel at Ampleforth Abbey on Easter Day 1994. Five months old, he fitted the embroidered christening dress easily. I was elegant in a hat and sweeping long skirt, proudly cradling my lovely infant son in his silk dress. The crypt was light with noonday April sun on this most gloriously hopeful Christian feast day. My friend John sang Schubert's *Ave Maria*, the priest used the words of an old Celtic prayer as he anointed Hal's mouth, ears, eyes, nose and hands with chrism for a blessing on the five senses. Afterwards there was a party: Easter roast lamb, chocolate torte, exotic fruit in technicolour slices, all my famed cookery skills to celebrate Hal's baptism. Pleasantly drunk, Father H. and Hal's godmother L. sang duets from Gilbert and Sullivan. And all was almost perfect.

Later I discovered that two of the guests had expressed concern about Hal to my mother-in-law R. One was a GP's daughter, thereby claiming some sort of authority in R.'s eyes, and she had said that his feet seemed very cold. Perhaps she confirmed R.'s own instinct that Hal was 'not right'. Both my parents-in-law had more or less avoided Hal from the moment of his birth neither touching nor photographing him. When T. was born, R. had marched in and colonised him; changed nappies, organised feeding and given unsought advice on 'routine'. When I balked at the word routine she replaced it with rhythm as if this simple application of newspeak would commend her view to my unthinking mind. She used to repeat the word, like a mantra as though it were part of some universally accepted body of dogmatic truths. By contrast Hal had been mine from the moment the midwife handed him to me. The reticence of my in-laws seems notable when I look back, but at the time I was delighted that I had a child who was mine, who had looked up at me wide eyed and terrified moments after his birth as though he was imploring my protection.

R. booked an appointment with a paediatric neurologist at St James's Hospital in Leeds and tried to persuade A. to take Hal along without my knowledge or consent. He refused, the first time he had ever rejected a suggestion by his mother point blank. We were allied against her bossy intrusiveness then, but still struggling to find a way of acknowledging Hal's problems to each other, and doing something to help him. Still wedded to the hope that Hal's problems were some sort of colic – though that hope was becoming faint by now – we took Hal to see a cranial osteopath. A gentle quietly spoken Canadian, he held the top of Hal's head gently and made infinitesimal movements. The next morning, Hal, who hitherto had always turned his head to the right in his bouncy chair, faced forward. It was a revelation.

The Bad News

When Hal was six months old he was referred to a consultant paediatrician at York District Hospital. By now we knew there was something wrong with Hal. He had not passed any of his developmental milestones.

The paediatrician came out to see us on a beautiful morning in June. He brought with him unannounced a student doctor. As I opened the door he said cheerfully,

"This is my student, do you mind if she sits in?"

Why didn't I refuse? Why did I say yes? Yes your student is welcome to witness your diagnosis, our shock, our grief. She is welcome to share the moment, observe our reactions, as if we were rats in a laboratory, then walk away.

Of course. Can I get you both a coffee?

The doctor examined Hal, tried to pull him to sitting, observed his head lag backward. Then he resumed his seat across the room, and after a weighted pause, he looked at A. then at me and made his pronouncement.

"I'm sorry, but I have to say that I think there is something seriously wrong with Hal."

So we received The Bad News.

Not Unprepared

I was not unprepared. I had read a great deal. I had been steeling myself for weeks, months. My fierce conviction that all human life was sacred – no matter how eugenically unimpressive – was about to be tested in fire. And I was shocked into a new reality, trying to take in the enormity of his words. So I answered his questions quietly and tersely – facile, pointless questions – about how this news made me feel. At that moment such questions were irrelevant. A. was cool and detached, his voice betraying no emotion, his features impassive as ever.

We were too calm for the doctor. He suddenly turned to face me and snapped, "You do realise that having a disabled child is hell, don't you?"

It was the tone of his voice, half angry, half desperate, as if there was something indecent in my failure to show my pain, and that if I would show something then his own anguish might be abated, that made me weep then and makes me shudder today. Perhaps it really is harder to break grievous news than to receive it. Perhaps the doctor needed to feel that he had done something to 'support' me at this moment of crisis and his statement was a way of jolting me into reality. It seemed to me like a gross intrusion into my privacy, a violation of my right to feel what I was able to feel at that moment. Evidently satisfied with the success of his gestalt technique he made a brief soothing noise and the student pulled a serious-mournful face of the kind newsreaders assume when they have a particularly ghoulish story to tell. After this they left.

I requested that Hal not be placed under this man's care, and resolved to find a different consultant.

No Ordinary Child

The day after this visit we went to the Ryedale Show. This is an annual event held near Kirkbymoorside which brings all the farmers down from remote farms on the moors with their heavy horses, prize stock, fruit flowers and vegetables, exotic breeds of chicken and ferret, all hoping to win prizes. I didn't feel like going anywhere, but T. was just four and the prospect of eating an ice cream, watching a gymkhana, and then eating another ice cream was his idea of a good day's entertainment.

The sky was heavy, promising the rain which is an inevitable feature of a country fair. As we prepared the children to leave, I contemplated Hal with a mixture of emotions. Can I recall and analyse them here? My predominant feeling was a curious one. It can best be described as an uncomfortable sense that I was deceiving people, betraying their expectations and beliefs. In an ordinary pushchair, dressed in ordinary baby dungarees, was no ordinary child. Here was an anomaly; not a sign of future joy, but a sacrament of the vanity and futility of human hope, the unfulfillable hope we place in our children.

Hal was, and still is, a beautiful child. Now I had to let everyone down; their pleasure in his beauty cruelly undercut by the reality of his condition, of which I still knew nothing.

We wandered around the showground in a daze. The tense thunderous weather mirrored my mood. I felt unreal, moving numbly, scarcely able to feel, except when I saw other children. Lively infants, plump and scrabbling at the straps which restrained them unwillingly in their pushchairs; grubby stumbling toddlers wailing for ice creams; children riding in the rickety fairground swingboats, faces gashed with screams of delight; children hurtling about the bouncy castle, crashing into each other and climbing to their feet without a second thought. Hal lay in his pushchair, uninterested, unmoved by the sights and sounds, stiff, his eyes dark with what seemed like fear.

How to do it? How can I be brave for my cheerful four year old stumping over the grass, pointing in excitement at the heavy horses, scrabbling down, and clamouring for another ice cream, another go on the swingboats? I clung to Hal's pushchair, wheeled him round and round the field until my head was spinning.

Gillian Upton Holmes

Changes, changes – an evolving diagnosis

Just over a month before my second baby was due to make its appearance in the world, the GP announced that he had found a spare head, and organised an appointment for me to have a scan the next week. This was a considerable shock – up to that point we had joked that the baby was either an elephant or a kangaroo because of its size and level of activity, but it had never occurred to anybody that a double bundle of joy was expected. After the confirmation that twins were on the way – any day – I spent the afternoon in a daze, trying to decide what extra equipment might be necessary, buying nappies, sterilising powder and a bucket (these were the days of terry nappies, and before scans were routine!), and telephoning the twins support group to try to access second-hand items. This seemed strange. As a health professional I had previously worked closely with the doctor who had had the foresight to set up the group initially, and we used to discuss the difficulties involved in bringing up "multiples." I had to get used to the overwhelming realisation that we were going to be a family of five, not four, and that there would be three children under two in the house.

A Considerable Shock

Three weeks later the twins were born and my older son and husband arrived in the ward. I shall never forget the reaction of my little boy. I had tried to explain that there would be an extra mouth to feed. At the tender age of 22 months he loved counting, and understood the concept of "two", but I was spellbound as he marched into the room and greeted me. He toddled to the cots, declaiming "Lum, doo", and looked inside, commenting with surprise, "Lum, doo baby".

My daughter's early days were marked by a breech birth and forceps delivery – an experience that caused my husband to be removed hurriedly from the delivery room because of his green face and wobbly legs – and a failure to breathe. The paediatrician, ("baby doctor", a term used by the staff, which I found rather insulting) seemed much more concerned about her clicky hips, than about my son's floppy tone and oddly bent feet. However, her subsequent development progressed along normal lines.

Voicing Concerns

Both twins were slow to grow, and we had to have them weighed weekly for a year. This entailed a fortnightly home visit by the health visitor, who was keen to assure me that breast-feeding twins was not a good idea, and that my son's development was fine, despite my concerns. Alternate weeks we had an outing to the baby clinic. This was up a flight of stairs in a church hall, and meant leaving the pram outside, picking up the twins, persuading my toddler to hang onto me, and making a slow ascent of the stairs. At the top, we balanced precariously on the final step while I opened the door with a handy elbow. We then descended the stairs at the other side of the door. Not a good experience, especially as it was punctuated by pronouncements that my milk was not sufficient for twins, and although I tried bottles as advised, both babies emphatically refused these.

The health visitor arrived to do a 6-month check-up. She insisted that I woke both babies to do this. As my son had been up all night, was not well, and had only just settled, he was not responsive. I was assured that, although she had previously felt that his development had been normal, she now considered that he had severe learning disabilities, and would not be educable. I was angry and frustrated. I had been voicing concerns about his physical and developmental progress while she had only focused on his small stature and slow growth. When I took him to see the doctor that afternoon as I had arranged, it turned out that he had measles. By then, the GP had referred my son to a paediatrician, and he was proclaimed to be floppy.

DIY NHS

From 8 months he attended physiotherapy weekly and gradually began to change from a rag doll to a baby who could sit up when strapped into a corner seat, with a table made out of a Fablon-covered whisky box. Do-it-yourself was also the order of the day when the physio had no splints to fit him, and I fashioned these from small washing-up liquid bottles, J-cloths and crepe bandages! Parents can be resourceful when problem solving. With hindsight I am appalled that the National Health Service was unable to provide splints, but I guess it contributed to my learning curve.

The physiotherapist and I became concerned that my son lost weight around his first birthday, shrinking from 13 pounds at 12 months to 12 pounds at 13 months. The paediatrician admitted him to hospital for investigations. This was complicated by the fact that I was still breast-feeding both twins, and there was only one cot available at the hospital. We therefore travelled the 25 miles each morning, arriving by 8:30 (the staff initially suggested 7:30!), complete with twins, camping cot kindly supplied by a friend, baby paraphernalia for two and harassed Mum! I paid someone to look after the older boy, who was still only two. The tests were inconclusive, but the doctor asked me to collect a faecal sample for ten days, not a happy prospect with a baby inclined to have diarrhoea. As the sample was borderline for coeliac disease, we had the delights of making a second collection. Life became dominated by poo, and trips to Scarborough Hospital to deliver samples to Pathology. My only consolation was that I didn't have to analyse the stuff!

Paradoxical Reactions

The outcome of all this was an admission to St James's Hospital in Leeds. I hurriedly weaned my daughter, as the staff refused to have her in with her brother. He was very upset by this experience, refused to eat, and the loud volume seagull-like crying he had had as a tiny baby returned. When given Valium to sedate him in preparation for his stomach biopsy, he became irritable and jittery, and his floppy muscle tone increased, to the extent that he pulled himself to standing in the hospital cot. At 14 months this was a first – even with splints, he found standing very difficult. From what I know now, the bowel problems and paradoxical reaction to Valium are indicative of his later diagnosis of an autistic spectrum disorder. When the biopsy proved negative, the doctor did sweat tests for cystic fibrosis, which were also negative, and the conclusion was that he had food intolerances – and it was a shame I hadn't fed him biscuits and chocolate, as these would have helped him to gain weight! I was quite taken aback to hear this from a dietician, but fed him the vitamins, iron and "Build-Up" as suggested.

My son continued with his regime of careful feeding and physio, progressed to playgroup and nursery, and remained an extra term in Reception at school. At this time he was seen by an occupational therapist, who, like me, was concerned about his behaviour as well as his physical difficulties, and suggested that I should seek a referral to a psychiatrist. The result of this was that I was given one appointment, at which I was told that my parenting skills were not adequate, and given several appointments (without my son) to discuss possible strategies. This was not particularly helpful, as I had already tried most of these ideas myself, but they did give me a chance to talk about my concerns – and reinforced my view that I was useless. I asked at this stage if my son had some autistic traits, but was told that this was not so, as he could speak. I was also informed that he was not hyperactive, because he had learning difficulties, and hyperactive children were bright. School referred my son to the educational psychologist, who said that he was to practise playing games in groups, and prescribed five sessions of group work. This was because he had the undesirable habit of wandering about, scribbling in other children's work, and ignoring his own tasks. At this stage, I was told by a doctor that I would not have been concerned about my son's development if I hadn't been a middle-class professional with two very bright children and one who was less able. This made me feel very small, and stupid.

All My Fault

At this point, I felt defeated. I had run out of coping strategies to help me deal with three young children, one of whom was definitely a non-conformist, was finding learning very difficult, and was always on the go. Despite his poor mobility he had become a little Houdini, escaping from pushchair, reins, and even clothes (not to be recommended in public)! I too was therefore always on the go, and tired and stressed, especially as our nights were still regularly disturbed by a little boy trying to climb out of windows (locked!) and to reach the front door key. I was now bringing up the children on my own. My husband subscribed to the view that there could be nothing wrong with his son, and that my handling of him was the problem. Hindsight now suggests that I was silly not to realise that it was strange that the other two did not have similar problems, but my self-esteem had taken such a blow that this did not occur to me. My former husband has only recently come to accept that our son does have difficulties, and still comments that I am over protective towards him. My daughter's view is that they have one parent who is over protective, and another who gives them far too much freedom. My older son declines to comment – but then he is a diplomat! I still feel somewhat undermined, because my younger son returns home from visiting his father announcing that he needs to be given the freedom to do exactly what he wants, as he is now an adult. Unfortunately his poor understanding of appropriate social behaviour means that he is vulnerable when not supervised.

No Action Taken

My next attempt to gain recognition of my son's differences and to obtain a diagnosis was at a case conference for another child, when I asked the occupational therapist to reassess my son because of his poor written work. I also discussed my worries with an educational psychologist, a former colleague who did not assume that single parenthood was a major contributory factor to his problems at school, and asked school if she could assess him. This resulted in my son being allowed to use a typewriter so that what he did write was intelligible, a great boon to him. The process of statementing started at this point. At the age of ten, his learning difficulties had been acknowledged, but there were a lot of minutes of meetings mentioning my concern about his behaviour, with no action taken. Typing lessons were also part of the statement – we're still waiting for those more than ten years later! Although school staff tried to be supportive, and positive towards my son, they were being expected to meet his needs without adequate resources. I was frustrated that individual support had also been withdrawn after a good year. This meant additional problems for him and a lack of progress the following year, when no individual help was offered. This seems to be a frequently occurring pattern in LEA provision.

The final year at primary school was punctuated by frequent episodes of difficult and awkward behaviour, for which I sought another referral to a psychiatrist. My son had developed several unwelcome obsessions, which made him very vulnerable in public. The psychiatrist again offered me some strategies for parenting, but felt that the behaviours were related to learning difficulties. My self-esteem plummeted yet again, and I can still be reduced to tears when the word "coping" is brought up.

Traumatic for All Concerned

Transfer to secondary school was very traumatic for all concerned, despite considerable support from the Special Needs department. By the first half term, it was obvious that individual help was necessary, and after receiving a detailed letter from me, the Special Educational Needs Advisory Panel (SENAP) agreed to provide ten hours a week (the norm was up to five then). I was somewhat upset by the missive received from the chief psychologist telling me that the extra support was being provided because I had written such an articulate letter. In my job I regularly write reports giving recommendations for support needed by children but the implication that children whose parents did not demand provision would not receive it disturbed me.

In the final term of the first year of secondary education it was clear that my son was becoming disaffected and stressed by the practicalities of having to cope with school. The main problems were a two-week timetable and the number of relationships to forge with staff. Then there was a hitch with navigating his way around the buildings to be in the right place at the right time – when less than ten minutes late, he was given a sticker, but had missed the beginning of the lesson, and never quite caught up. He was unable to write down homework from the board quickly enough at the end of lessons, so would be in trouble for not doing the work. A lot of letters and phone calls were generated! For me as a professional visiting that establishment to see youngsters with speech and language difficulties, and thus needing to liase with the school's Special Needs Co-ordinator, life became quite complicated. We had a weekly meeting when I went into school, at which I wished to discuss my clients. However, the SENCo was glad to have an opportunity to speak to me about my son, which I found awkward, as the transition from therapist to parent and back again was quite a stressful switch. I did request a chance to come in on a non-working day but this was not convenient for the teacher, and so did not happen. I appreciate that teaching staff are busy, but it really would have made a significant difference to me. I had been able to negotiate separate days for appointments at parent consultations for the twins at the primary school, which had been successful for me. It is not easy to talk about one child who is making good progress and then launch into a lengthy discussion of the other's major problems, or vice versa.

Weekly Boarding

My son was very fortunate in being offered a place at a school for dyslexic boys, at which he had to board during the week, as it was 70 miles from home. True to pattern, he accepted the major change to boarding without turning a hair. The main problem was that he had to wear new grey trousers instead of black ones, and a grey jumper rather than a maroon one! He particularly liked the headmaster because at his interview, the head showed him the school ducks, and called him "sweetheart"! Although this teacher had been a colleague of mine several years before, I found it easy to separate friendship and parenthood – Rob called me "Mrs. X" when he was being the Head and my christian name at other times. This was his way of handling a potentially complicated situation, and worked well for me too.

This school offered my son a number of opportunities he would never have had at a mainstream school. He learned to canoe, ski, climb, abseil, did his bronze life-saving award, and, best of all, could camp out in the grounds in the summer. The staff maintained a routine, and care and teaching staff worked closely together, giving clear expectations of what was required. The boys were taught in classes of up to eight, and – another bonus – were encouraged to let off steam by BMX biking round the grounds at break time. Because my son did not sleep very well, and was often found wandering about at four or five in the morning, one of the care staff used to take him for a run every night, and introduced him to fell-running. His sleeping patterns improved considerably, a rare example of a behaviour that transferred from one setting to another without having to be taught. The fact that my son was away during the week meant that his brother, sister and I at last had some respite from him, and we could do activities together that he would have disrupted. An added delight for me was that his handwritten work became legible, and he enjoyed learning, as school recognised his learning style and tapped into his interests – a lot easier to do in a small school of forty-five boys than in a comprehensive school.

And Finally

By the time my son was fourteen, he had had some extra diagnoses – dyslexia (or specific learning difficulties) and dyspraxia, and another doctor had assured me that he had neither attention deficit hyperactivity disorder (ADHD) nor autism. I felt sure that he had Asperger syndrome (an autistic spectrum disorder in which ability to learn is within normal limits), and spoke to my son's school GP, who referred him to the psychiatrist. Unfortunately I also mentioned another syndrome I had heard of, and the referral was passed on to a paediatrician and then a geneticist. No diagnosis was given at that stage, but a couple of syndromes were ruled out. As my son was now fifteen and due to leave school the next year, the school GP kindly sent a referral to our local learning disability service. Following three assessment sessions the clinical psychologist was able to refer him on to adult services because he was almost sixteen. We were very fortunate in coinciding with the window in time in which there was a locum psychiatrist who was willing to make a diagnosis of Asperger syndrome and she threw in a label of ADHD as well. This took place two months after my son's sixteenth birthday, making the acquisition of a diagnosis a very lengthy business, as concerns had been present since his birth. Although there is now a greater awareness of Asperger syndrome and ADHD, sadly my experience is still not uncommon.

Gillian Payne

Pioneers

Supporting a child is a hard road
Life with our children is comparable to
a journey through the Himalayas
without any boots:
the lows are lower
the highs are higher;
the pain is deeper and
your feet hurt.
But the views are worth it.

A Mum

2 So What's Wrong With Him?

My Life is Just My Life

I prefer kid's attitudes to adult attitudes because at least they ask straight questions and offer honest answers. Adults tend to talk in a roundabout way but I don't really care, I'm not bothered anyway. My life is just my life.

One little girl once asked me in a quiet, curious, thinking voice:

"What's it like not being able to walk?"

"I don't know really, I don't know what it is like to walk."

She seemed satisfied by this answer, unlike her mother who looked very embarrassed, rushed up and dragged her bemused daughter off in a heap. See what I mean?

I felt very comfortable with the little girl's open honest approach. The mother on the other hand left everyone present feeling just as uncomfortable as she did and missed an opportunity of learning from her daughter.

The other day a little boy, Ben, really made me laugh. He said in an inquisitive voice, as he looked at my legs in my wheelchair, "Do you have any knees?"

That really made me laugh, fortunately his parents weren't there to spoil the experience. Why can't adults just lighten up and see the funny side? Why have they always got to be so bloody serious?

Children always approach me very naturally and look into my eyes and talk to me simply, with openness, and naturally treat me as they find me. Adults, on the other hand, have to work very hard at being natural; it seems to be something they forget after puberty. They try to hide their inquisitive glances but I instinctively know what is going on inside of them because I recognise what is going on inside of me. People just don't seem to get this. I am perfectly happy with my life. I can't imagine what it is like to have your life. I am not a victim. Yes, I have to plan how to access buildings but I can think for myself when people let me and if they won't let me, tough, I'll do it anyway.

A Young Person

The Gossip Witches

The gossip witches never stop talking about you. Every sharp, sly word is another ice brick in the wall between you – and your fearful state – and their safe, warm, comfortable lives. The gossip witches sit in their covens, Wednesday afternoons over tea and wicked cream cakes, weaving cocoons to keep them and their children safe and clean. Spinning spells to ward off taint.

Four hundred years ago a child who was different in some way was called a changeling. The fairies had spirited away the real child and left in its place a strange, deformed, odd creature, the changeling.

What is it the gossip witch fears? Abnormality, taint? Does she think that if she ostracises, mocks and blames the mother of a child who is different – who is impaired – that the fairies will spare her own precious darling, not steal it and replace it with a changeling?

Or is it the typical behaviour of crowds? The playground huddle of backs as you creep along the wall, holding your breath with fear?

Do they enjoy their scorn? Am I, to them, less than human? A scarecrow, an Aunt Sally, a scapegoat, to jeer at for a moment then pass on?

But are not they me too? Because I have known the gossip witch in myself. Before the painful time of reckoning, before the shock of a truth that laid open my heart, before the cocoons that shrouded my soft life were ripped from me. How often then in that soft life did I laugh and gossip and pick over the individual tragedies of people I scarcely knew?

Hurt makes us open our hearts and our arms to those who have been hurt too, at least for a while. None of that cold hard striving is lost. It is part of the anatomy of compassion which enlivens and empowers. Pity on the other hand drains all the life from what it touches. Pity truly is of the devil.

I think I believe this. Misunderstanding, unkindness, thoughtless cruelty, somehow makes us stronger. In the mysterious economy of the universe, evil diminishes when suffering is transformed to strength.

Gillian Upton Holmes

Unhelpful and hurtful comments

They said: Maybe he would be better dead

They said: Put him in a home and get on with your life

They said: At least you have one son who is normal

They said: How good he was born to you – you will know how
to look after him

They said: At least he didn't die in hospital

They said: Good job he's underweight – won't be so heavy to lift
and carry

They said: Forget your tears, get on and look after your
children; think of them not yourself

They said: Make sure you have time for yourself

but they never,

not once, not ever,

offered to help or have any of the boys.

Lesley

The Making of Me

Everyone wants to feel included, to belong and to contribute to any group in which they are involved, be that a family, school, club, or team at work or play. In this piece I describe how my own experience has influenced my attitudes towards disability.

An Unusual Background

I have always felt strongly about inclusion. Coming from an unusual background, I have always had to make an effort to become and feel included. My parents were British but lived in a North American university community, alongside people of diverse nationalities and interests. They had friends from all over the world. The Second World War had not long since ended and my parents' friends included people who had lived in concentration camps, displaced persons' camps and in countries that had been overrun by Germany or Russia. These men and women were pursuing academic careers and, like my parents, becoming accustomed to a new culture, and learning to understand each other's ways.

Mum and Dad spent each summer travelling, complete with army surplus tent and kids, to conferences all over North America. This gave me and my sister a wealth of experiences. We met rattlesnakes on a field trip to the desert, dug for clams near Seattle and went onto the Athabasca Glacier by Snowmobile. We visited pueblos in New Mexico, learning that not everyone had a tap in the house. The chief really was called "Running Water" because he did have piped water. At that same pueblo I discovered adults did not always understand the lifestyles of others – two ladies walked round and round the beehive oven in the centre of the village looking for a way to turn on the electric power. I guess it showed me that not everyone had the range of knowledge I took for granted.

Tolerance and Acceptance

My childhood experiences laid a strong foundation of tolerance and acceptance that I draw on in my working life as a speech and language therapist and as a parent of children with disabilities.

It certainly influenced my choice of Speech Therapy as a career. I searched the library to find a job that combined an interest in languages with working with people, and found speech therapy in a chapter on social work. A neighbour, who was a headmaster with a disabled daughter, introduced me to the local clinician, and I was offered some observation sessions. I also helped at Brownies as a "pack leader", and subsequently a "Tawny Owl", and as a patrol leader at Guides was entrusted with some of the more difficult girls. The leader thought that I would be able to get them to join in with the activities of the group.

I could probably do this because during my childhood I often felt left out. I had considerable problems with co-ordination; for example I had never been able to crawl, and as a baby was unable to hold my bottle. My parents arranged for me to see a paediatrician, who suggested that I should wear specially made shoes. They also encouraged me to attempt many physical activities with other children, but I was frustrated my inability to keep up with the others and eventually refused to join in. We moved house several times, and I had been at four different schools by the age of seven; two were in America, with a rural school in Oxfordshire and a bilingual one in Paris sandwiched in the middle. In Paris I lived with a French family, good friends of my parents, while Dad was working in Sweden. When we returned to California I was put in a class with children a year or more older than me. In fact, having an August birthday meant that there was almost two years' difference in some cases, which leaves an enormous gap in social and emotional development at that age. I was also one of the smallest in the class – I didn't actually realise that this was related to the age gap. I wore glasses and, for a while, a black eye-patch, which led to my nickname of the "pirate kid."

Back to England

When we moved back to England, I was just eleven, and started secondary school at the right age. The P. E. teacher noticed my clumsiness and arranged "deportment" classes before school once a week. This meant walking around the school gym miserably failing to balance a book on my head and learning to swing my right arm forward when I moved my left leg and vice versa. I still catch myself getting the pattern wrong. I was also enrolled for elocution lessons, partly to increase my confidence, and partly to remove my American accent. Some pupils and members of staff initially found it difficult to understand my accent when I arrived at the school. I was not accepted into the choir because I did not pronounce "a" correctly – a clear case of discrimination and lack of inclusion. This would not be a problem nowadays, as children are exposed to American cartoons from an early age. England was generally more insular in the Sixties! Now that I live in Yorkshire my "a" fits in perfectly with northern English.

When I applied for speech therapy courses I hit a problem. School felt that as I had academics as parents, I should go to university. However the only degree course in speech therapy required a science "A" level, and I was doing French, German and Music. The headmistress hauled me out in front of the whole school in assembly to berate me for not completing a university application form. My parents both backed my choice of career. Given school's desire for a "proper" higher education, I did apply to become a teacher of deaf children, and to study linguistics, as well as to the one speech therapy course. I was offered places at each of these, the last subject to taking Biology "A" level. However, as I had been offered a place at Jordanhill College in Glasgow to study for a diploma in speech therapy, I did not go to university. Now all therapy courses are degrees, and my diploma is accepted as an equivalent qualification. My languages and music have been important in my career. I have given therapy in Russian, translated in French and German, and the auditory discrimination skills practised in music have honed my ability to listen.

College life suited me, and I enjoyed the practical and theoretical aspects of the course. I was able to establish relationships with my Glaswegian relatives, many of whom I had never met before. Social life was busy – I sang, played the guitar and piano and joined the Christian Union, as well as working very hard. My ambition to join the college orchestra as a cellist was thwarted, because rehearsals always coincided with clinical placements.

Starting Work

My first job was a generalist post. I worked with all ages from a six month old with a cleft palate and feeding problems to a ninety-six year old who had had a stroke. I was involved in setting up support groups for patients who had had strokes, and one for their relatives, and another for laryngectomees. I also worked with people with voice disorders, and children with cerebral palsy. The Cerebral Palsy Unit was attended by children with other developmental and learning disabilities and the occupational therapist, physiotherapist and speech therapist worked as a team. We ran groups for children and their parents, or saw individual youngsters. I also helped to run an evening class for people who stammered. The department worked closely with an Audiology Unit, where children with hearing loss or severe communication difficulties were assessed and treated. This gave me a first experience of teaching sign language.

After two years in this post I married and moved to York. My job there was again varied and included three special school sessions. The new boss was apologetic about this, as previous therapists had not been keen to work in special education. I loved this work, and soon acquired three further sessions in a Language Unit, later becoming the senior therapist for special education. I added a school and hospital for people with severe learning and physical disabilities to my caseload. In this setting I became a tutor for the Makaton Vocabulary Development Project. This meant that signed communication could be used within the hospital environment. The clinical psychologist and I carried out a research project on the effect of using signing on the comprehension of people with learning disabilities.

A Full-Time Mother

After two and a half years in this job I left work to become a full-time mother. My older son had advanced language development, but poor speech because of a significant level of verbal dyspraxia (a difficulty in co-ordinating and sequencing speech sounds, although all the sounds can be produced in isolation). We worked together to good effect on his speech. As an adult, he still speaks fairly slowly, especially when he is tired. It also takes him much longer than others to complete written work, but given extra time in exams, this did not stop him coming out of university with a good degree.

I had been a parent for almost two years when "mother of three" and "mother of twins" superseded the tag "mother of one" on the same day. That maternal role has probably been the most important and exhausting of my life, with innumerable rewards and a few sorrows.

The twins were diagnosed late, but arrived safely. The first had a normal delivery and a floppy body, and subsequently failed to thrive. His twin sister arrived one foot first, almost half an hour before the rest of her appeared with the aid of forceps. She did not breathe immediately, and had "clicky" hips. She was smaller than her brother, but grew and developed normally despite the difficult start to her life. The months sped by in a flurry of feeding, sleepless nights, nappies, washing and, above all, my new son's seagull cry. This was recognised by all the other mothers in the main ward, and the ward sister christened him "the demon" because of the volume and piercing nature of his screams. This cry continued to punctuate the days and nights for his first two years. Friends at Mother and Toddler Group, church and even the local shopkeepers came to recognise the sound of his approach. I was concerned, as I was aware that an unusual cry could be related to disabilities, and watched and waited, observing his development minutely. I was not reassured. Our difficulty in establishing a diagnosis is discussed elsewhere in this book in "Changes, changes, an evolving diagnosis".

His sister also bore the brunt of the problems in school, as staff used to summon her to sort out any inappropriate behaviour shown in class or in the playground, caused by his social difficulties. She did not often invite friends over because of him and at home she also had to cope with a very stressed mother. She insisted on attending a different secondary school, at which she did well. She also sheltered me by not mentioning the level of her interventions on her brother's behalf until recently. This seems to be a common pattern, with siblings taking on enormous responsibility.

Serendipity

Once my younger son had been diagnosed with Asperger syndrome (an autistic spectrum disorder in which ability to learn is within normal limits) and ADHD (attention deficit hyperactivity disorder), there was little medical follow up. His education fell into place, albeit with a degree of serendipity. When we had concerns about a particular aspect of his development or learning, doors seemed to open. For example, he was offered an early nursery placement because of his developmental delay and physical difficulties. He was given an extra term in a reception class with a very experienced teacher, who then stayed with his class in Year One. After I mentioned my concerns to the educational psychologist following a case conference about one of my clients she went into school to discuss my son. She arranged for assessment of his needs, which led to a statement of his special educational needs, and extra support in class. My son's secondary school posed dilemmas for us. We debated a placement in a school for boys with specific learning disabilities (e.g. dyslexia), and, after a difficult first year at mainstream secondary school, he was offered a place there. He later attended an Independence Unit at a local special school, where he thrived.

At the age of eighteen he was offered a place at a specialist college for young adults with Asperger syndrome but funding fell through and he went to a college for young people with moderate to severe learning disabilities. His interpretation of the situation has had a profound effect on his acceptance of his difficulties; he feels he cannot have Asperger syndrome, or he would have been sent to the appropriate college, and has never come to terms with this part of his diagnosis. More positively, he used to be quite discriminatory towards those with severe learning disabilities, and at college he learned to get on well with a wide variety of young adults and now values them as individuals. The care side of the college was mainly good but the academic aspect was a disaster. He was moved from campus to campus and was therefore unable to complete courses. He also had some time (with inadequate support) at two mainstream colleges while still based at the residential placement. I spent a lot of time trying to explain how important consistency was to my son but the college staff did not seem to appreciate how unsettled and insecure he was feeling. People with autism find change difficult. When my son is upset or anxious he tends to compensate by becoming over-familiar and boisterous, which the college interpreted as meaning that he was happy. I find it alarming that a specialist college is so lacking in awareness about the fundamental characteristics of autism.

My son has now spent eight months at home attending a sports course at a mainstream college. There is a good support network, based on recommendations from him and me, and he is coping with travelling twenty miles each way every day. The course tutor was initially apprehensive about including him on the course but says that, despite some initial difficulty in settling in (particularly over-familiarity with staff and girls) he is now accepted and included as a member of the group. He is now working towards a Level 2 NVQ, demonstrating what can happen with the right support and attitude from well-trained staff and careful collaboration and planning.

Relishing Independence

He, with four others who also require support in daily living, has recently become a tenant in a house run by the Wilf Ward Trust. He has settled well – in fact, he is reluctant to come home for visits because he relishes his independence so keenly! The staff members are able to persuade him to do things that he considers mere parents should not demand of him.

He also has a hectic social life, both with the others in the house and within the community. He is working towards his Gold Duke of Edinburgh award, attends a lively special needs youth group and a church youth group each week, an activity scheme in the summer holidays, and is a member of a dramatic society. To facilitate these activities I have frequently been called upon to offer transport, a role recently acknowledged by him when he presented me with a “Mum’s Taxi” car sticker. Now that he is in his own home he is within walking distance of more of these activities, which has changed my life considerably.

His future plans are not decided. He is a good swimmer and holds a National Pool Lifeguard Qualification. He would like to work in this area and is currently seeking a work experience placement. Given his difficulties with concentration and social communication, he would require a high level of preparation and support, which is hard to set up. This is the next challenge and battle for recognition and acceptance in the world – one needs to be realistic and optimistic, and find appropriate compromises and suitable mentors and role models, not an easy order to fulfil.

I returned to work when my children were five and seven years old with a new fund of experience to draw on in my work. Because I had first-hand experience of the lack of support available for families of children with special needs I decided to join a pilot group working towards a parent-led support facility in Ryedale which became Ryedale Special Families. I am still involved with the organisation as a Trustee. The long attempt to find the right education for all my children meant I wanted to see children achieve their potential and find their niche as mine had done. I was determined that other children and parents would not have to face so many problems.

Gillian Payne

Before David

Before I had my son David I had not thought very deeply about people with disabilities beyond a vague and distant sympathy. Sympathy for them, their half lives and for their disappointed parents and carers. On occasions there was revulsion, and a lot of ignorance. I think this is simply an attitude I learned growing up. I remember a big, hulking, lumbering boy in grey shorts and long socks in my early childhood, Ian. I have no idea what his disability was but I do remember we kids kept our distance. He wasn't at our school. There was pity for his long-suffering mother.

Usurping the Proper Baby

I also remember as a child listening to grownups talking about a recent birth. To my young ears, listening carefully to the hushed tones, it appeared that the subject of their conversation had not had a baby. Instead she had had a Mongol. In my imagination this was a curled up, cowering deformed little creature that had usurped the proper baby. A few years after this, I recall Mum telling me that apparently we couldn't say Mongol any more; it was now something new, "Down's Syndrome". Twenty years later when my son was born with Down's Syndrome an elderly and very kind friend reassured me that it could have been worse, I could have had a Mongol.

I don't remember anyone with disabilities at school and this is highly likely to be because there wasn't anyone. They were probably in special schools. As many of my generation do, I can still picture the groups of child adults on a trip out holding each other's hands and wearing frumpy dresses, cardigans and knee high white socks.

As a Girl Guide part of my "Service Flash" award was spent visiting a home for the mentally and physically handicapped. I certainly felt very noble, kind and worthy going to minister to these poor souls. I was very uncomfortable at a surprisingly good-looking wheelchair bound young man with some mental disability chatting up my sister with a twinkle in his eye. This certainly did not fit my picture.

I found it hard not to be repulsed by the dribbling and the inability to eat "properly". I'm ashamed to write that, but even now my better self cannot override some baser distaste at lack of control of one's body like this. As a teenager I would sit at the tea table with my Grandma and Great Aunt, both of whom I loved, forcing myself not to look at the food dribbling from the corner of their mouths.

There was a partially sighted student on my course at university. He had to hold things incredibly close to his face. His eyes rolled, and he had a mini telescope to hold up in lectures. He was very clever, but he didn't look it. And I remember with shame giggling at him privately with my friends, one of whom could do an impressively accurate impersonation of him.

Of course, publicly I was as politically correct as the next young idealistic liberal student. I could talk the talk, make the donations, sign the petition and make sure I met the eyes of the person in the wheelchair, not just the person behind pushing. But I note with interest my chosen "good works" at university. (Good for the CV). Many students got involved with working with mentally and physically handicapped kids. I didn't. Instead I went to visit a mentally ill woman at the local mental hospital. I think I felt that somehow this was more worthwhile – after all there was always the possibility of really helping someone like that. They could get better. You could recover from a mental illness couldn't you? But not from being a spastic or deformed.

Keeping My Distance

I think I have grown up not wanting to dig too deeply and explore my attitudes. Disability was not something I could comfortably classify and accommodate into my worldview. Certainly in my younger years I very much needed the security of order in the world around me and in my head. Disability seemed some kind of aberration, a malfunction of the human species. So I chose to ignore as much as possible and keep my distance.

Not until my son David was born did I have to seriously confront my feelings and attitudes. I would like to be able to finish this piece neatly and tell you that I have done a complete U turn as a result of knowing David, but I can't.

He began the process of eroding prejudice, preconceived ideas and most of all fear. He replaced them with love. But I worry that the channels he opened will begin to silt up again. After all, he was only ever a baby. Everything he did was cute and babyish. All babies dribble and drool their food. All babies need nappies, have little control of their movements, cannot talk properly and are prone to make loud incomprehensible noises at inappropriate moments. I never got to find out if I would be able to cope with this when my son grew from cute baby to disabled child.

I have many, many regrets that my first born son died so young, at 13 months. One of them is that we did not have long enough together for Mummy to enter more fully into the world of disability. A world of challenge, contrast, conflict and pain; but also of joy, simplicity and a whole new outlook on life. A world briefly glimpsed, a brief sojourn. We did not have enough time, David. Not nearly enough.

Sue Smith

Special – why special?

Around the time Hal was diagnosed and I was hovering outside the gates of The Great Disability Industry plc, I was sent a leaflet by social services. The cover read:

My child is ... special

I know. I know. Whoever wrote those words was trying to be sensitive, trying to empathise. Trying to do all those caring things that social work training had prepared them to do. But it made me mad. So mad that I picked up the phone immediately, unthinkingly (a mistake as usual), and vented my spleen on the hapless receptionist at head office. This is how parents of disabled children get a reputation for being ... difficult.

Now I know my reaction might seem a bit excessive, yet I am increasingly uncomfortable with the language used to describe disability. Euphemisms (or politically correct terms) have to be revised again and again as each successive word acquires its own negative connotations. During the ten years of Hal's life he has been disabled, differently abled and with special needs. He has had specific difficulties, non-specific learning difficulties, severe learning disabilities, additional needs and profound and multiple learning disabilities. On being informed of this, ordinary people ask me what's wrong with him.

To outsiders the abundance of terminology leads swiftly to a loss of meaning. This is ironic since one of the things we on the inside want is inclusion in the ordinary world. "Learning disability – is that what I used to call mentally handicapped?" wails my husband and laments that he has been alive so long that he no longer remembers which terms are polite and which are offensive. I adapt my terminology depending on my audience; spastic (which describes Hal's disability precisely) is simpler than spastic double hemiplegia with profound and multiple learning disabilities in reply to a polite enquiry from a slightly deaf (or hearing impaired) lady at the church fete. I have a lot of sympathy with those disability groups in the U.S. who have reclaimed the word 'handicapped'.

Language has a Life of its Own

I've heard the arguments against the term handicapped (coming from the phrase 'cap in hand' it implies that all disabled people are beggars) or spastic (a playground term of abuse). I've read the earnest promotional literature from national organisations of disabled people ("Don't say wheelchair-bound, say wheelchair user"), but the idea that you can change attitudes by changing language is at best naïve and at worst sinister. I don't think anyone will understand Hal better by calling him a 'wheelchair-using person with cerebral palsy' rather than a 'wheelchair-bound spastic'. No, it ain't what you say it's the way that you say it. I remember my mother losing the plot in the early 1970s; she was completely uncertain about the politeness or otherwise of 'nigger', 'coloured' and 'black'. Now nigger has been expunged from the vocabulary of all polite liberals, yet even as I write this, the word is being reclaimed by young radical rap artists and has long been part of the language of the ghetto. Language is like this. It has a life of its own. The same fate will surely befall the words currently viewed as acceptable. 'Special needs' already has a similar flavour as 'handicapped' and 'subnormal' had when I was a child thirty years ago. Meanwhile the response of individual people to children like mine is as unregulated as ever.

The word special has its own ugly history. The first occurrence of 'special school' recorded in the Oxford English Dictionary is in a tract of 1908 called *Mental Defectives*. So here is 'special' right at the heart of the eugenics movement which generated fear of disabled people, particularly those with mental disabilities, by a theory of contagion. Francis Galton, Charles Darwin's cousin, invented the term eugenics and his ideas were enthusiastically taken up by British intellectuals including George Bernard Shaw and H. G. Wells. The weak, the feeble, those who were unsound in mind and body were a threat to racial strength and purity, fit for special schooling and other special treatment. In America 30,000 mentally disabled men and women were castrated or sterilised by 1940. Under Nazi rule in Germany, abortion to eradicate hereditary disease and disability was mandatory from 1935, and in 1940 a euthanasia programme for killing disabled people was implemented (it was called *'gnadentod'* – mercy killing). Under cross-examination at Nuremberg, Dr Karl Brandt, Hitler's personal physician, admitted that 60,000 people had died between 1940 and 1945 including senile patients and children. In Sweden, young women with learning and other disabilities were subjected to compulsory sterilisation as recently as 1976. Today, the withdrawal of medical treatment from severely disabled and sick babies and adults makes regular headline news.

The eugenics movement casts a long shadow over families with a disabled child. And belief in eugenics is not something we can safely consign to the past. We are not meant to give birth to 'defective' children any more in this brave new world of prenatal testing, ultrasound and genetic science. Eugenics is still with us, and because of this the disability rights movement has some serious arguments with genetic research. The real argument is not with the scientist's quest for truth, but what we do with this new information. Now that we can have so much control over our genetic future, what decisions should we make and using what moral framework to help us decide? It is hazardous to simply accept that 'the doctor knows best' and as families with disabled children we are the poor bloody infantry in this particular battle.

Talking to Ourselves

It often seems to me that the disability rights movement hasn't yet made much impact on the wider world beyond those directly concerned with living and working with disability. It often feels as if we are talking to ourselves. Out there people carry on understanding disability through their own private definitions. While we may see disability as no more than a variation of the norm, they may well see disease, and they persist in their individual responses, indifference, pity or hostility.

Often writing or thinking about disability, I feel that I need a more profound language. A language which moves beyond the jargon, the medicalese and the shallow civil rights speak. I want a language which can express the subtle gradations, the interstices of who and how a person is, when that person is physically dependent and does not speak.

In the play *A Day in the Death of Joe Egg* by Peter Nichols (himself the father of a severely disabled girl) the central characters Brian and Sheila play games, act out scenes, give their daughter Jo a set of personalities. Jo is a blank: brain-damaged, cerebral palsied, cut off behind a wall of medication and tangled neural connections. For me, the play raises an important question – how far do we, the able and active, impose our own constructions, our story, our version of who our disabled children are?

A Poetics of Disability

When Hal was tiny and I first came into contact with the experts in all their array of knowledge and methodologies, I was confronted with ways of describing reality that were radically different from my way of seeing, describing and therefore of perceiving. The scientific approach – tabulate, formulate, compare, distance – has its own beauty, but I feared its crudeness. I feared that the moments when Hal comprehended or responded would be crushed by the therapist with her tables and the paediatrician with his charts.

I needed words to describe a response or a fleeting comprehension gone in a moment. I needed a language and a grammar to give structure to the person I knew, to his being and my relation to him. A poetics of his disability rather than a science.

By giving myself permission to understand him in this way, I reclaimed him from the experts who knew so much more than I. They knew about his condition, but I recognised him. They were professional; I was triumphantly amateur, his mother. I like the word amateur, with its roots in the Latin word *amare* – to love. Yes – my child is special, but special according to *my* private definition. The word special is reclaimed for the lexicon of love.

Gillian Upton Holmes

3 My Life is Just My Life

What Happens to the Families of a Disabled Child?

The playwright Peter Nichols wrote of his play *A Day In the Death of Joe Egg* that the problem is not only how to live with a handicapped child but how to describe that life in a way that will prevent a sudden stampede to the exit door. Adversity either pulls people together or tears them apart. You may be familiar with the book *Women are from Venus Men are from Mars*, and when a disabled child is born the differences between men and women become very clear. Having a new life to care for is in itself an exhausting task but when your tiny offspring is disabled that task becomes even more demanding. Mothers have a strong instinct to nurture and protect. I found it impossible to 'switch off' and in a way I resented my husband's ability to do just that. I felt sure that when he walked out of the door in the morning, to go to work, or out of the door in the evening, to pop up the road for a pint, he was doing just that. I'm sure he must have felt the onerous responsibility of bringing up a disabled child but I'm convinced it isn't a constant in his life.

Guilt, Energy and Switching Off

Any mum will feel guilty taking time for herself – we know we shouldn't but it is very hard not to. There is a lot of guilt where disability's concerned and it's a very destructive emotion. It gnaws away at your self-esteem. You lose interest in so many things. There simply isn't the time for the superficial – it does not seem important to do your hair or put on your face. How hard for someone to come home from work and be greeted by a woman he barely recognises. How hard to be that woman, who barely recognises herself. This is where marriages sometimes begin to break down. You simply feel as if you haven't the energy to maintain the relationship.

'Going out' comes very low on your list of priorities not least because baby sitters for disabled babies and children aren't easy to find. I was lucky that my parents lived nearby and were wonderful with Tom and James, although it wasn't always feasible to leave a baby with a metal bar between his legs in the care of others. There were good friends, special people, to whom I entrusted Tom when I needed a break to recharge my batteries but in reality I never "switched off" completely. We managed to maintain some semblance of a social life. Friends and relatives continue to include Tom in their invitations.

Muddling Along

When Tom, in his teens, went off to College over two years ago my husband and I should have been able to pick up the threads but it didn't happen. My husband had developed a male-orientated, squash playing, rugby watching, pub visiting social life that I couldn't be part of. I enjoy my own company and have become used to travelling alone. I suppose circumstances dictate how marriages evolve. People change, I certainly have, but adjustments are made. Couples learn to compromise as marriages move into other phases. In middle-age there is pleasure in those social occasions where good friends meet to celebrate anniversaries and birthdays. There is so much delight in the renewal of old acquaintance and sharing of memories. Affection comes in many guises, there is still comfort in that which is familiar, the key in the lock and the creaking stair on a dark, cold night. So marriages muddle along, sometimes in the most extraordinary way.

Guilt is often accompanied by anger, which can be so easily misdirected. Sometimes it's those you are closest to who are on the receiving end. And in a family there are so many roles and relationships to take care of beyond that of husband and wife. There are your parents and in-laws, your brothers and sisters and, most importantly, any other children in the family. I would have liked to know how to help my able-bodied son, James, grow up as Tom's brother. I'd like to share with you James's thoughts about this.

When I asked James to pass on some of his thoughts about growing up with Tom I was surprised by some of what he had to say. I had not been aware of it at the time. As a small child, Tom was unintentionally sometimes very destructive and the distress for James was palpable when his precious artwork was destroyed in seconds. James learnt to have eyes in the back of his head. He said that because caring for Tom was mentally and physically difficult for me it made me "very high maintenance", as he put it, which didn't help my relationship with his dad. Children are unhappy when their parents don't seem to be getting on well together. But mostly James looks on life with Tom as having been a positive experience. It's made him much more patient with those less able but paradoxically less patient with those who can help their behaviour. In times of stress when the going gets rough for James he says he thinks of Tom and that helps him put things into perspective.

There was never any sibling rivalry or envy on Tom's behalf. It saddens me that James feels the guilt too. He saw the differences between himself and Tom as some form of injustice, as if there were a set of scales and all the good fortune had been heaped on his side. As he says, this wasn't a very constructive viewpoint for him. Sadly, he says that from a very early age he found it difficult to believe in God. Despite this, to me he epitomises a true Christian and respects all religious beliefs. It seems ironic that I have a twenty year old son who doesn't believe in God and an eighteen year old who still believes in Father Christmas.

Not All Doom and Gloom

If the picture I've painted seems somewhat bleak, I'd better redress the balance because having a disabled child in the family isn't all doom and gloom. But there are times when you do hit rock bottom and your personal reserves run out. At times such as these, when crisis looms, to have the support of a parent-run organisation such as Ryedale Special Families providing a shoulder to cry on, gives an emotional release. Within the company of those who've 'been there too' it becomes easier to cry and laugh and pick yourself up off that metaphorical floor and carry on. Very often all you can do is 'carry on'. The problems of living with the complex needs of our beloved disabled children do not go away.

I've always liked the oft-quoted expression 'A man's reach should far exceed his grasp' and I've tried to keep this in mind for Tom, too. When James was a child, he and I decided it simply wasn't fair to leave Tom behind and sneak out of the house so we could go riding. We determined to break James' pony Toby to harness and take Tom out with us into the countryside to enjoy the wildlife. This gave Tom so much pleasure. As time went on, we taught Tom to ride too. What wonderful freedom that was for us all. We were a familiar sight in Thornton le Dale either riding or in our pony and trap setting off for picnics in the forest. Tom was unable to walk far because of his clubfoot so we would carry him from the trap and sit him down under a tree by the lake in Dalby while James caught frogs and newts to show him.

Big brother James continued to be a terrific support through the years that followed. Life without him would have been much duller for Tom. I could rely on him in the most practical of ways. James enabled me to fulfil a promise made to Tom when he was barely ambulant that to celebrate his eighteenth birthday I would take him on safari to Africa. As this date drew nearer it seemed a daunting proposition but promises are promises! In the middle of the Masai Mara when a 'comfort break' involved using what was basically a hole in the ground surrounded by a picket fence James's sense of humour and hands on approach to caring relieved me of the duty of seeing to Tom's most basic needs. To travel through the savannah alongside huge herds of wildebeest, zebra and elephants with a disabled young man was not for the faint hearted but what an amazing travelling companion Tom proved to be. In the company of his zoologist brother James we were thrilled to encounter a pride of lions after they'd feasted on a buffalo kill. The tiny cubs wandered around our stationary vehicle showing intense curiosity as Tom fearlessly clicked his camera button! The two couples travelling with us told us that having Tom on the journey had enhanced the whole experience for them. We seem to meet delightful people on our travels.

We continue to travel, last year journeying to Seattle to visit James and enjoy a whole month in America. My husband, Phil, flew out for two weeks. We stayed at a wonderful inn below the Cascade Mountains. James and his wife Julia and members of her family joined us on many occasions ensuring the Fletcher family had the holiday of a lifetime. Whilst we were there Tom and I took an Alaskan cruise which proved to be a wonderful experience. Again, we had terrific travelling companions. Friendships were forged through Tom's capacity to connect with people. His fascination with other cultures brings joy to those who meet him. He has danced with the Masai at a bush barbecue on a pitch-black Kenyan night and with Tlingit Native Americans around a fire pit in Alaska and as long as my bunions and Tom's club foot will allow us to we will hobble up aeroplane steps and respond to the lure of other continents.

Libby Fletcher

Written by A Mum

Being a 'Mum' is the most wonderful thing that any woman could wish for. The first sound of your child's cry makes your heart miss a beat and the bond begins.

However, being the 'Mum' of any child, disabled or not, is hard work, stressful and extremely tiring. The tantrums of early toddlers to the teenage 'strops' are all part of them growing up. My youngest daughter finds life hard, surrounded as she is by a disabled family; therefore she is very insecure and has difficulty in detaching from me. She still cries sometimes when I go out which I do very little (she is ten years old). My eldest daughter is fourteen and has learning disabilities and is very insecure and needs lots of input, attention, assurance and love. My partner has Asperger syndrome and depression and is harder work than the children.

Anonymous

In This Together

From the very beginning, when I was struggling to conceive, Matt and I made a conscious decision to work together. When I fell pregnant with Charlie that decision stood.

The first week after Charlie was born we were staying in the hospital in a parents' room near his Intensive Care bed but after the week we had to hand the room over to another family and begin the daily journey from our home, a very long 156 mile round trip through the East End of London. I was offered a single room in a hostel near the hospital but it was never an option. We again chose to travel every single step of this journey together. It was a decision that I believe saved us. I feel very fortunate as I write this six years on.

We were told about, and experienced many times, the damage that the enormous stress of having such a poorly baby can cause. A consultant informed us one morning, whilst performing his daily rounds, that the divorce rate of families who experience a baby cared for in Special Care was over 50 per cent. He then went on his way as usual. Matt and I just looked at each other, half shocked by the statistic, half bemused at the way in which it had been delivered to us.

Unfortunately we went on to discover the truth behind the statistic. We went on to watch three families separate within the first three years. All three blamed the stress that their unexpected role as parents of disabled children had brought to their lives. Watching families break up was very sad, and each time made Matt and me more determined to stay together.

Don't get me wrong: there have been many occasions when we wondered if we could possibly carry on. Matt walked to the front gate many times, as did I; but we would take deep breaths and walk back in. Five minutes in the cold air, usually about midnight, always seem to help.

Still to this day as much as possible Matt and I attend most of Charlie's hospital appointments together. One year Matt used all of his annual leave on days at York District Hospital and Leeds General Infirmary. We combine the appointment with lunch out or a trip to the park and talk about the consultant's words. For us it has been a combination that has worked. I felt very aware that, as much as I was the one who contributed to this book, we are one unit, with Matt very much the silent, but always the supportive partner.

Heidi Ridgewell

Mothering Sunday

Give mothers tools.
Tools to save their children,
Not to dig their graves.
Give mothers hope.
Hope to see a future,
Not hope that lives will end.
Give mothers dreams.
Dreams that show tomorrow,
Not dreams of yesterday.
Give mothers flowers.
Flowers for a dinner table,
Not flowers for a grave.

Libby Fletcher

From Diaries/Journals Kept

1992 George One

Knocked sideways. The walking dead. Cold Dark Despair

Abyss Abyss Abyss. Dreaming. Nightmare. Fear Dread Anger. Drowning Drowning Drowning. Alone and Lonely. Nobody knows!

Will the sun ever shine again?
Will I ever laugh again?
Have I any tears left to cry?
Where is God now?

1993 George two
Charles three + half

Living gets no easier. I put on my mask and go through all the motions every single day. Why are professionals so unhelpful? They remove the last dregs of my self worth. I am a Nothing caring for a Nothing child. Why does no one or nothing come to my help? I feel so terribly, terribly guilty. I do not want this son of mine who is more like a doll than a living child. There is nothing there – Help me someone – soon.

1995 George 4
Charles 5 + half
Harry born

What a traumatic year. Can I go on feeling so depressed and desperate? I have had Harry to try and save my marriage. Am I a fool? Maybe. George recognises me and I feel very protective over him. Charles is an unhappy schoolboy. Harry is a crying, difficult, baby. My husband is no help. I feel so ill physically, mentally and emotionally yet the days pass by with no regard for me and my difficulties. I am unimportant to life.

1998 *George seven*
Charles eight
Harry three

Have slowly been finding myself, hidden away for so long. I get glimpses of my old self. I look in the mirror and see myself looking back at last – how old I look – how old! I asked my husband to leave. I ended my marriage. I feel a great weight has lifted. It was the right decision. I no longer feel I should just put up with everything because I deserve it in some way. I do not deserve it! Has all this really come from just having a child with disabilities or is there more to my reaction?

George and I have a wonderful relationship. He is my tonic, my inspiration. Strange how that has changed. So, I feel myself very lucky at having experienced having and knowing this dear (obstinate) boy.

2001 *George ten*
Charles eleven
Harry six
Mum forty-five

Strands of life coming together. I feel more of a whole not a million fragments. Ten years of our lives gone. Has it been wasted? Who can judge? Who knows? I have learnt to sit lightly on things. I have learnt to love in a different way. I have learnt so much through the last ten years. I take each day as it comes (or try to). I have a lot on my plate and am grateful for it all. I have concerns for George's future – whatever will he do? Who will care for him? Will they treat him right? Will he be abused? Will he live? Will he die? Which is really worse?

Lesley

Confessions of a Working Mother

In 1980, ten weeks before my first son was born, I left my post as a Senior Speech Therapist for children with special educational needs to apply myself to the job of motherhood. This I found to be a pleasant experience, as Richard was an amiable baby, who enjoyed adult company, but could also entertain himself. I was amazed when I noticed that at the tender age of one month he was able to select the correct movement to operate his Activity Centre. He really could aim and move his fist vertically or horizontally to make the spinners go round. With this first baby, I had time to interact socially with friends who also had young children. We all had husbands who thought we would be grateful to change from paid professionals to mothers/ domestic engineers/Jills of all trades. Our group of six young Mums went on to have second babies – or in my case, twins. We continued to meet socially, although the frequency of our gatherings decreased as we moved house, or gradually took on part-time work as nurses, teachers and speech therapists.

The Job of Motherhood

I was the last to return to an official job, although while my children were at Toddler Group a friend and I became responsible for starting a second session as numbers expanded. I kept my speech therapy hand in by working with my own children, two of whom lisped, one also having a moderate degree of dyspraxia (difficulty in co-ordinating and sequencing movements). The third's speech and language was within normal limits for a twin. Ironically he was the one who had special needs, including delayed physical development, failure to thrive, ADHD (attention deficit hyperactivity disorder) and specific learning difficulties – and autism!

While the children were at playgroup I assessed several children with speech and language disorders and the local speech and language therapy manager regularly briefed me about extra jobs which might materialise in the near future. When the twins started nursery, I spent one afternoon a week working with adults with learning disabilities, and a second teaching lip-reading – again unpaid, but I gained valuable experience by doing this. I was also able to assist the Speech Therapy service by seeing two children with severe speech and language difficulties who attended the same nursery session as my offspring.

In the term in which the twins started full-time education, a part-time job was offered to me. Three mornings a week was ideal for a return to work. Unfortunately as I had not worked for seven years, I had to start again on my career pathway, at a basic grade. This was frustrating, as I had been a senior therapist in the months BK (before kids). However, as I was the only candidate for the job, I was able to negotiate to work during term time only, and take unpaid leave during school holidays. This was a first for our department, and I am grateful that the manager sanctioned my request, as fifteen years ago, carers' needs were not always considered important.

"I" not "We"

As the children grew, I was offered extra days at work, and found an excellent childminder, a former nursery nurse, who had known the children since my older son was at nursery. This meant that I did not have to explain my younger son's odd behaviour to her. He also knew that she was "to be obeyed", and her consistent handling of him resulted in good if somewhat lively conduct most of the time. This childminder was also rather special in waiving the retainer fee and letting me pay just for the times the children were with her. This was a particular boon, as shortly after I started to work – and incidentally this coincided with my becoming more assertive – my husband had left, announcing that he could not cope with stress at work and at home. His rationale appeared to be that if he moved out he would be able to continue to work, and could therefore carry on with some financial support for the rest of us. I am still uncertain how he felt this would leave the rest of the family, with a mother working part-time as well as dealing with three children, one of whom had considerable physical, learning and behaviour difficulties. This separation occurred shortly after our younger son had been referred to a child psychiatrist because of his behaviour problems at school. I remember a psychologist who assessed him at the same time commenting that when talking about my son I always said "I" rather than "we", and having to explain that his father was not very closely involved in issues of parenting.

The next challenge of being a working mother was coping with mumps, chickenpox and "Germy Wheezles" (my son's terminology!), which all three had in rotation. Fortunately some of this spate of illnesses coincided with school holidays and visits from relatives so babysitting problems were reduced. One of my non-working friend's children were also being daubed with calamine lotion because of "chicken-pops" (another new word from my son), and she welcomed my spotty small fry, who arrived with cotton wool, bottles of calamine lotion and packed lunches. This was a blessing, as the childminder could not have them at her house with her other healthy charges! I guess it was the equivalent of the "measles parties" my mother and her peers arranged, although the purpose of those was really to try to expose all the children to the bugs. I did have to cancel some days at work to fill in gaps in childcare. Unlike teachers, speech therapists don't often get supply cover. Obviously children's illness is a problem that arises for any working mother, but with doctors' and therapy appointments as well it is even more of an issue for parents of children with disabilities.

Trying to Change Hats

When my son was assessed and received a statement of special educational needs we had to attend numerous appointments – mostly on my days off. When he was at secondary school it was hard to maintain a barrier between work and home life, as I was going into his school to see other children, and the special needs co-ordinator wanted to speak to me about his difficulties as well as those of my clients. This I found extremely hard. I had always tried to attend parents' evenings at primary school separately for each of my own children, as a means of coping with the difference in their abilities and successes in class. Trying to change hats between discussions has always been hard to do. However, the up side was that I was treated as a partner in the decision-making process around my son, as the teachers and educational psychologist knew me as a professional as well as in my role as a parent. Mind you, it is hard when wearing the "parent" hat to challenge the plans of professionals with whom you will have to work the following day. I sometimes imagined my life as tightrope walking while juggling job, family and home, uncertain if the safety net was present, and unable to look down in case I lost my balance. This feeling never goes away.

I requested an interim review at school because I was concerned about how traumatic my son found his own juggling experience at secondary school. Because he finds it hard to organise himself, he was very often late for classes. This meant that he would often miss the first few minutes of the session, and thus the explanation of what he was supposed to be doing. At the end of the class he would not have finished writing down his homework before the rest of the pupils left for their next lesson. He would then forget which room he should be heading for next – or get lost on his way. There was a two-week timetable to cope with, and when he got home there were partial instructions for homework, and demerits and detentions for not completing the set work correctly. His behaviour at home suffered too, and he became disaffected at school, needing considerable encouragement to attend. This caused a great deal of pressure on the whole family, and my concentration on my work also suffered.

As a result of this, I wrote to the education authority to ask for support in class for my son, which was given “as a result of my eloquent and articulate letter.” This made me angry, because it implied that children of parents who accepted the status quo, or did not know the procedures, would not be able to access appropriate support. At the end of the year we were lucky to be offered a place at a school for boys with specific learning difficulties. This was a real help to the rest of the family. I felt extremely guilty we were so pleased he was to be a weekly boarder, but we all needed some respite, as his behaviour at home had become so disruptive, and his lack of sleep meant that none of us were functioning very well. He had been damaging or hiding our belongings, something that still happens when he is anxious or stressed. A particularly annoying example of this was his habit of changing the clocks so that they all showed different times. This again had an impact on how I coped at work, and I was feeling upset that other families seemed to be getting more support than we were.

No Real Problems

At this stage, one of my friends suggested that my son was probably eligible for Disability Living Allowance, and I applied for this. Until then, I had been told that he had no real problems other than my perception of him, and so assumed that he would not be eligible for benefits. In fact he was granted the higher rate of Care Allowance, which confirmed my anxieties about his development and behaviour. No professionals had ever discussed access to benefits for my son, and some expressed surprise that he was awarded them.

My son settled well at his new school, and life became easier as the other two children were able to spend time doing activities of their choice rather than having to consider their brother all of the time. The extra space meant that we were happy to have him back at home each weekend, and tailor the days to his needs. There were several traumatic incidents, such as having to deal with two fractured wrists, and weekly visits to the hospital to get the plasters replaced after a week of hard wear at school, followed by a round trip of 140 miles to restore him to the school. I *knew* there was a good reason to avoid working on Mondays and Fridays!

Although my son is now 22, I still work part-time, as he finds it hard to cope with college holidays. I normally enjoy being able to spend the time with him, although he feels frustrated that I am unwilling to leave him on his own for a whole day at a time. He prefers to spend time on his own at his father's house, because he has a computer, video, DVD player, and ghetto blaster at his disposal. If I am at home, he will often telephone me by 9:30 asking me to collect him and take him out for the day. I have taken him to Scarborough on the pretext of going "shopping" so that I can fit in a school visit or half a day at a staff meeting, but he was once sick, and now refuses to be left on his own in town in case it recurs. As he is most likely to be sick when anxious, this restricts my attempts to work during holidays. There are some activity sessions that he can attend in the summer, which gives me three days of work between 10:30 and 3:30. However, as he becomes anxious about getting to the meeting points on his own I have to build in extra time in case he requires transport – as the sessions are often twenty-five miles from home, this cuts down still further my time at work. The other strategy he has used is to appear at the office of a local charity supporting families of children with special needs to offer his help. This is just round the corner from his Dad's house – but I always feel guilty when I find that he has approached the office, as he can be rather disruptive when he is not the centre of attention, and likes to talk at people. He does not know when to stop because of his poor awareness of non-verbal cues. I suspect members of staff are too polite to feed back their needs for peace and quiet to him. I find college holidays extremely tiring, and become very stressed.

Not So Straightforward

Here is just one example of how something apparently straightforward can become a problematic issue for my son, and therefore for me. This occurred one holiday. There was a stomach bug going round the students and, as nobody living in his house had contracted it yet, I was asked to collect my son on the Wednesday morning. He phoned me on the Tuesday evening at 11:30, complaining that the staff had told him to pack, but this was too early, as he was not due home until the Friday. I assured him I would be coming to Lincoln the next morning, but was unfortunately delayed in heavy traffic, which upset him – he likes things to go according to plan. On the way home, I explained that because I had an afternoon meeting in Scarborough I would therefore leave him at home. He became distressed and refused to be left, as he was not yet supposed to be back. I therefore took him to his father's house – as that had not been part of the plan, this was acceptable! On the Thursday I phoned to ask if he wanted to come home, but he hesitated, and said it was not the correct day. He was happy to go on an outing, and did come home for a meal. However, all the way through dinner, he was worried about when he would get back to his father. On Friday morning my son and his bag arrived on the doorstep at 7:30 – he'd been nagging his dad to give him a lift, as it actually was Friday, and he was supposed to be home. This is not an isolated incident, but it gives a small illustration of how unsettling it can be for someone with autism when plans are changed; the level of anxiety must leave them feeling constantly insecure.

I think guilt is probably an emotion experienced in liberal measure by all working parents, and it is certainly one well known to me. My boss has been very supportive of my role as a working parent and, because I have ensured that most appointments with my son have been arranged for non-working days, she has given me carer's leave when necessary. I now work half time all year round, but do extra sessions within term time to make up for the times I am not able to work during my son's holidays. However, because I am now also doing some locum sessions when I am available, I feel guilty when these have to be cancelled in order to transport my son to college.

Getting it Exactly Right

I am fortunate in having reasonable health, but because of the pressures of home and work, life has become increasingly hard to balance in recent years. The transition phase of my son's education, and planning for his future have definitely taken their toll on me, to the extent that I now suffer from anxiety and depression. This necessitated my having to take six months' sick leave, which increased the burden on my colleagues – more guilt! I have managed to get back to work but I still find it difficult. If I have had a stressful time with my son I cannot easily switch off. There have been major difficulties in sorting out arrangements for my son's college education, and his levels of anxiety have increased. This has necessitated a lot of negotiation with college staff. I have been frustrated that the college has not been sufficiently aware of the implications of their decisions on his behaviour. This has led to additional pressures on him and on me. A considerable proportion of my non-working week has had to be spent in liaison with college. I am proud that their reaction is now "I'm glad you phoned, because I wanted to run this idea by you before we change his timetable" rather than "I suppose you might as well come for a face-to-face meeting as you'll be collecting him on Friday."

However, this has had an effect on my work. I become agitated about report-writing, as I am so aware of how important it is to get it exactly right to avoid the problems caused by the lack of information submitted about my son in the past by fellow professionals. This means that writing has become a complex and painful task for me, and I often end up in tears of frustration – possibly "anguish" would be a more appropriate word to use in the circumstances. I am also perpetually physically and emotionally drained, with disrupted sleep patterns. When I get home from work, I often sit down and fall asleep, waking at two in the morning, or occasionally not until the clock radio rouses me when it is time to get up. This means that work suffers. I also feel frustrated that because of the size of my caseload (over 200) I am unable to support families and children as well as I would like to. At least I can empathise with parents of children who are having problems at school. Of course this becomes a vicious circle, as I feel so strongly that I would like to ensure that children are helped to reach their communication potential.

My other frustration is that I am still working as a fairly junior therapist, despite having worked in a specialist senior post before having a family. I have had to make a lot of compromises – but I am happy that I have been able to continue working despite being the mother of a young person with disabilities. I am glad that I made the choice to work part-time while my family was growing up – but I never expected to have a son of 22 who is still so dependant on me, or to be a part-timer for so long!

Gillian Payne

Bustin'

Who designs disabled loos? Clearly not disabled people. Now, you may think this is a funny subject to want to write about but, believe you me, if you were disabled and you needed the loo you would want this matter raising because you would already know many disabled loos are 'no go areas' for wheelchair users.

Let's look at the obvious. Which section of the community are disabled loos aimed at? Physically disabled, of course. But many loos are not big enough to fit a wheelchair. Now, if the disabled person could walk and leave the wheelchair outside we wouldn't have a problem because then we wouldn't need disabled loos at all. Everyone could use the existing ladies and gents. This is all starting to sound rather ridiculous. Can somebody just tell loo designers to please design wheelchair accessible loos big enough to actually take a wheelchair? To the few designers who have successfully designed large, accessible loos please ignore this and accept my heartfelt thanks.

While I am on the subject, and for some amazing reason still hold your attention, could we also have overhead hoists fitted please? In all my years of caring I have only ever found one toilet with an overhead hoist. Well, at least it is a start. Change comes slowly. I sometimes feel as if we are facing a long uphill road all the way. I hope there is an accessible loo at the top.

A Mum

Beware

When life is applied using pressure through wheels, not feet, be aware of the 'no go area':

Steps
Stairs
Steep inclines
Uneven ground
Sand
Soil
Gravel
Narrow spaces
Rain (jams up controls)
Toilets, even some disabled toilets.
Cars, buses, trains, planes.
Houses with steps.

I remember a kindly helpful person once said to me
"Oh yes, we have a disabled loo.
Just over there,
Up the two steps".

A Mum

My Special Children: a conversation with God

I suppose you said typical when I tried so ineptly to tune in for a chat, one of thousands round the world who, when the going gets tough, expect some sort of help. Maybe you didn't receive my signal or chose not to respond to it. Well, I did need to speak to you and once or twice I thought you'd heard my pleas but the reply faded away as if you didn't understand my language or I didn't merit a response. Was I being presumptuous in an attempt to understand your great plan? Did you have a quota to fulfil – for every 100 or 1,000 or 10,000 perfect babies did one have to be disabled? How were Tom and I chosen to be the 'special' ones?

A Malicious Game

Are there pros and cons or do you simply spin a wheel? Did we just happen to come up *numero uno*? I'm aware of my imperfections but I thought no one else was. You, of course, know all about them and maybe you felt I deserved this special need's baby. What a cruel irony that my second special need's baby veered towards a different end of the spectrum to my first. Were you playing a malicious game, taking delight in building up and knocking down us humans and our search for perfection? The perfect wife, the perfect marriage, the perfect home and finally the perfect family

Were you listening when I tried to speak to you? I suppose you were, even though you didn't seem to be when my baby bleated painfully and plaintively for succour and I could give him none. I was forced to withdraw my instinctive response, the one that came from deep within my belly, where it pummelled in my gut until I felt numb. Sometimes not even a sip of water passed my tiny baby's lips for fourteen hours. Does he remember in the deepest part of his subconscious, perhaps, a mother who failed to meet his needs? Well, I remember and there's my hell.

Sorry

I'm sorry if this conversation is beginning to sound like a diatribe. 'Sorry' is a word that features heavily in my vocabulary. It was the word that pounded in my brain when I handed Tom over to theatre staff, who sometimes returned him later with the announcement that "he'd been too snuffly to anaesthetise". That was the worst: 'Make another appointment'. For more torture? Nearly always last on the theatre list 'dirty pot, infection risk to other patients'. Well, that didn't placate me and I committed a heinous crime. I showed my emotions. I cried. Was this when medical staff labelled me 'emotionally labile'? I remember an irritated doctor snapping at me,

"Look, he's forgotten all about it now he's got his bottle!"

Was I wrong to cry?

Twenty years ago, when Tom's orthopaedic surgeon held that tiny deformed foot in his hand he told Tom it was a cruel world. He turned to me and spoke with a directness that most doctors seem afraid of. We spoke the same language. What a relief to find someone in this nightmare world I'd entered, after days of agonising labour, who spoke to me as if I could cope with the truth. When I finally returned to the world, after my pethidene assisted labour, and was handed the tiny baby who'd refused to enter this cruel world without the intervention of forceps, my remark that Tom had a club foot was countered by the nurse.

"It's just the way baby's been lying in the womb. Anyway we don't call it a club foot these days, it's known as Talipes."

"Call a club foot a club foot."

That is what I'd say to her now. He was tiny, he was incomplete and I was numb. I was taken to the maternity ward where I was able to witness the joy that should have been mine in the eyes of the other mothers. When Tom refused to suck from his bottle my concerns grew. I asked the nursing staff if my baby had suffered brain damage.

"Oh no, Mrs Fletcher, he's had a trying delivery."

So I fed him by tube. It was all such a blur. If only there had been more honesty, fewer platitudes and less condescension from the nursing staff. Perhaps their training is to blame? Do you remember me trying to bargain with you, or am I just one of the many mothers of disabled babies who offer you everything and anything to make it better?

Tom Didn't Complain

Tom's orthopaedic surgeon described himself as a carpenter, a truly cruel irony don't you think? My image of him, saw in hand, is actually very close to the truth. At times, medical intervention felt like an act of enormous cruelty towards Tom. Throughout it I functioned on autopilot, a coping mechanism common to all those Mums who face a lifetime of caring for 'Special Needs' children. But even this could not block out a terrible anxiety about whether the pain Tom endured could ever be justified. I aided and abetted in the many surgical procedures and operations Tom underwent feeling guilt ridden for the cruelty inflicted on my son. Sometimes it seemed the operations were performed for Tom's benefit and sometimes for the benefit of medical research. Tom is now 21 and his withered and scarred leg culminates in a small battered appendage barely resembling a foot.

During his years of NHS treatment Tom didn't complain. He stoically endured so much, his sweet nature endearing him to those who looked after him over so many years. I was also sustained by rare moments of morbid humour. I remember his carpenter surgeon turning to the paediatrician and declaring:

"This is the mother and father of a club foot. I shall take this to my grave with me."

The reply came back,

"I suppose you'd call that 'one foot in the grave'."

Laughter and Anguish

I bet you understood why we were laughing. But did you also understand my anguish when my angelic baby lay in my arms and the carpenter strapped the Dennis Brown metal splints between his tiny fragile limbs? Back then, I didn't realise this battle with nature would continue for more than a decade. The doctors didn't look beneath my brave face. Did you? Not that my brave face was a permanent feature. I'm no hero, no saint, but of course you know this. I'm not super mum, never have been. Only you knew how much pain and depression filled my daily life.

When I finally took my tiny baby home I had to adjust to another professional: the Health Visitor. They were mostly interested in weighing Tom, who had to be weighed inclusive of the ironmongery attached to his feet by strapping. It gave clinic and health visitors an extra calculation when they checked his weight to see if he was 'thriving'. I soon resorted to shrugging my shoulders when people enquired how much he weighed. Visits to hospital to restrap his splints were dreadful for Tom. When the strapping was removed from his legs it also removed his paper-thin skin.

It was such a relief when Tom was given his first white leather boots with open toes. No more strapping, thank goodness, just a screw hole in the base of the boot so the ubiquitous metal bar could be bolted between the feet. At last the pile of tiny socks could be delved into. Tom started to play with his toes lifting feet and bar in the air then clanging them down. Changing nappies was easy, bar and legs were lifted in one action as the nappy was slipped underneath. I wonder if Tom felt manacled by the tortuous bar, even though his sunny disposition allowed him to smile and chuckle. But you would know, wouldn't you? I didn't have time for intimate conversations with you over the next few years. I didn't have time for anything much beyond coping with day to day existence.

Juggling

We moved to the impractical four-storey house that we'd agreed to buy before Tom's birth. It had endless stairs, a kitchen in the basement and a funny sort of shed type bathroom extension on stilts, which the wind whistled through in winter. The view was beautiful but there was no time to stand and stare. I started to decorate with a vengeance. I wallpapered the lofty Victorian dining room, working until late at night, with Tom and splints propped in a tiny baby chair at the foot of the stepladder.

I muddled along clinging to what normality I could, juggling the needs of my eldest son James with those of Tom. This got a bit easier when three-and-a-half year old James began attending a small convent school with the neighbour's children. Religion became a hot aprés school topic and my concern that he would be brainwashed by Catholic beliefs was unfounded. When one of the sisters told him the devil made it rain he was quick to retort that it was actually God who gave us rain so that the flowers could grow and the grass could grow to feed the animals. James was his own person, a feeling he had exuded from the day of his birth. When he was born I was stunned by his dark all-seeing, all-knowing eyes and when I held him and looked into those eyes it was as if I was holding someone who'd been here before.

I was happy that he loved every minute of his little old-fashioned school and this made it possible to give myself to Tom in his absence. Life was hectic, punctuated as it was by endless visits to the professionals. Throughout Tom's life the list of people involved in his care grew like Pinocchio's nose! Portage and the health visitor came to the house. Portage isn't professional advice on how to lift and carry your disabled child. It gets its name from a town in Canada that pioneered this form of support. It consists of a peripatetic teacher who visits the home and involves parent and child in a range of activities to stimulate learning. I bought a beanbag to plonk Tom and splints on during the day. The health visitor quizzed me on his slow development, but the issue of his foot seemed of overriding importance at this stage. I wondered if the portage teacher was achieving anything in the way of stimulation. I shared my fears with no one and held them deep inside of me. I wasn't aware of you as I hauled myself through days of tedium and exhaustion, all the while trying to retain some degree of composure.

Nil by Mouth

James's teacher started to pray for Tom's foot, which though it seemed a futile gesture curiously gave me some comfort. I wasn't aware of your presence on the dreadful days when Tom went to the operating theatre. The torture inflicted on my tiny baby began the night before. My guilt stays with me to this day. I would feed Tom to the terrible ticking of the clock until 'midnight – nil by mouth' arrived. I'd put him in his cot, lull him to sleep whilst his daddy was at the pub and older brother asleep. Please don't wake Tom! Rigid in bed I'd listen to my heart beating until I fell into an awkward half sleep that let me stay tuned in and waiting for the cry that would propel me from my bed. Here is a pattern for life set fast. Demons still crawl from the pit of my stomach through the long dark hours to torment and challenge me. I still leap from bed when a breath of a breeze stirs the branches of the plum tree outside Tom's bedroom window. Of course you know this, you were there too.

How do you feel when you hear the hellish cry of a baby pleading for milk and see a mother desperately trying to stifle her instincts? There should be an edict that states: 'Thou shalt not conceive and give birth unless you are prepared to inflict heinous cruelty upon your greatest love'. Did you hear my silent cries, did you hurt too? Do you remember the long, long nights becoming bleak grey mornings? Waking James quickly, praying he would rise without waking Tom if he was still asleep. James was dropped off at Nan and Grandad's so we could leave for hospital with our fractious baby cradled in my arms. Every twist and turn of the car journey was as familiar as the walls of our home. We'd reach the ward, go through the heavy doors that swung back on us, and I continued to cradle Tom against the cruel world that awaited him. The cruel world the carpenter had spoken about on the day Tom was born, the day he'd declared what a challenge Tom's clubfoot would be.

Over three years we moved from splints onto tendon operations. A long incision was made down the back of the leg, then the tendon was cut and stretched and rejoined before the cut was stitched up and the tiny limb encased in a plaster cast from toe to knee. After recovering from the anaesthetic Tom and I would return home. I wonder if observing the pain, discomfort and distress that Tom endured was the beginning of James' compassion for all things living? My 'bright star' appeared to be unaffected by my absences with Tom. The deformity of Tom's foot seemed fairly inconsequential to James. He loved Tom – splints, pot legs and all – but I'm sure his disabilities did affect James' life. Perhaps they are partially responsible for forming the person he is today.

A Gifted Child

When our little Convent school closed I knew James needed the continuity of primary education. Initially the headmistress at the local primary school announced that at four-and-a-half he was too young to be enrolled but eventually she capitulated. He hadn't been there long before his teacher was eager to inform us we had a 'gifted' child. It gave us a frisson of delight but I wondered if this was an intervention on your part, to balance the scales. On the one hand, I had a beautiful healthy and gifted son and on the other a beautiful son with cerebral palsy, severe learning disabilities and severe talipes who, we would in due course discover, also had severe eyesight problems. There were too many days when I felt guilty about not being able to be there for James because Tom's needs were too great. My parents gave James that 'other home' when I had to be absent with Tom.

None of us will ever forget *The Birthday.* It was February. Ice and snow had hit North Yorkshire, roads were blocked and I was preparing treats for an after-school party for James and his friends. The WI lady knocked on the door and delivered the cake decorated with a pony to represent James' beloved 'Toby'.

Tom was grisly, which was so out of character, and he had been like this for a few days. That morning he'd cried when I'd put his boot on his little foot, as we now called it. The foot had ceased to grow properly due to the operations. I felt under the foot and found a swelling. When I pressed it gently Tom screamed with pain and I immediately rang the surgery. A doctor agreed to see us at once. During the previous operation, Tom had had three pins placed through his apology for an ankle. The plaster cast had been replaced over a six-month period and on the final pot removal the pins were also removed. The GP looked at the swelling

"It appears to be an abscess but I'm reluctant to interfere with it. I think you had better take him to Outpatients at Scarborough Hospital".

Husband Phil was out somewhere on the North Yorkshire moors doing a survey and uncontactable. I rang my parents and as luck would have it my brother was visiting. We transferred James' party food and goody bags to mum's and bundled the now screaming Tom into my brother's four-wheel drive vehicle. On the road out of Thornton le Dale towards Scarborough there was a backlog of vehicles defeated by the icy conditions. We were lucky and made it up the hill and finally reached the hospital where we took up residence in the dreary old fashioned outpatients. I tried desperately to calm my now distressed and screaming toddler as my brother fumed.

"I wouldn't let my family endure this", he muttered.

No Solace

Angry looks and glances from irritated patients had little effect on me. My mind was in two places, here with Tom clawing at my shoulder in desperation and in Pickering where James would be excitedly gathering up his friends in anticipation of his birthday party. I fervently hoped my parents would be able to cope with a small mob of unruly little boys and girls and willed James not to be too disappointed. When we were finally ushered in through the serried rows of exasperated outpatients, I was resigned to the ghastliness of the situation.

Once inside the carpenter's inner sanctum I collapsed into a chair with my demented child. Tom's surgeon recoiled in horror as he examined the foot. I'd always spoken frankly to this man, as he had done to me, and I believe we respected each other for this. I think he said 'What have I done?' before informing me that at the last surgical procedure he should have removed three pins and had only removed two. A metal pin had been left in Tom's foot.

"Perhaps you need a holiday, like me?" I said.

"No," he replied. "I need to learn to count to three."

I didn't berate him, I didn't rant and rave, I was simply too exhausted. I merely asked, 'What next?' Tom was sent for x-ray and then admitted to the Children's Ward.

By the time my husband appeared later that evening, Tom was back from theatre and coming round from the anaesthetic. The dreadful pin, which had been working its way gradually out of the foot and caused such intense pain when pushed back in by boot or pressure, had been removed with ease. Tom's temperature was returning to normal and we would be able to take him home later that night. It was way past his bedtime when we collected James from his grandparents. When I finally fell into bed I couldn't have been at a lower ebb. Once again I was unaware of your presence. I felt so isolated; there was no solace, just autopilot.

The Living World

When James was six we moved to Thornton le Dale to a more practical three-bedroom house. We had stables for the horses and pony; a lovely enclosed garden and, joy of joys, a downstairs loo. Life at Thornton le Dale village school was for the most part idyllic and James thrived in the atmosphere. Excellent teachers in a lovely environment with a terrific close-knit group of friends gave James all he needed at this stage.

We acquired a trap for James' pony Toby so that Tom could enjoy outings with James and myself into the countryside. By eight, James had become an avid naturalist, rescuing injured wildlife and becoming a member of the British Trust for Ornithology, with whom he started to train as a ringer, and assist in providing data for national surveys. He raised funds for a local wildlife sanctuary by raffling a watercolour painting he produced of one of their residents, a peregrine falcon. Tom delighted in the enchanting world that James opened up to him. Rescued tawny owls came to live with us and later a barn owl. Unable to be released into the wild, they enhanced the restricted world Tom lived in. Though Tom continued to receive "Portage" it seemed that interacting with the living world was more stimulating and certainly more enjoyable for him. He also enjoyed visits to the speech therapist at Pickering Clinic and I left these sessions if not optimistically then with a feeling that all was not doom and gloom.

When Tom was given a place in the nursery over eight miles away the morning sessions he attended should have given me some respite but the reverse was the case. By the time I'd taken him there, in a borrowed car, and returned home there was little time for me before I had to make the return journey. I tried to give quality time to James, too, but found myself increasingly exhausted with the demands of a routine that kept me constantly on the move.

Your Grand Plan

At Thornton School James was just one of the gang and his emerging talents were no hindrance to him at this stage. When he was given the opportunity to play the cello he was ecstatic and by the time he moved on to the local comprehensive school he was identified as being musically gifted. Whilst he was playing at a musical workshop, I was approached by a distinguished elderly gentleman with a long flowing beard. He suggested that James would benefit from a specialist musical education such as that provided by Chetham's School of Music in Manchester. Was this delightful man part of your grand plan? If so, it was a beautifully engineered move on your part. After auditioning within the hallowed medieval walls of Chetham's School of Music, which sits in the heart of Manchester within a stone's throw of Victoria Station, Boddington's Brewery and Strangeway's Prison, James was offered a place. There was little time to contemplate the pros and cons. Christmas was on the horizon and the Director of Music suggested James should become a pupil at the beginning of the next term in January.

James was thirteen and for the most part was coping well with the curriculum at school. His school cello lessons, though, led to conflict with the sports master, who insisted he attend all sports activities despite James only being able to receive cello tuition when the peripatetic teacher visited the school. This, of course, coincided with some sports periods. James loved sports, he was an excellent runner and cricketer, but he was driven by a passion to play the cello. His sports master insisted that sports should take precedence over music and James was on the receiving end of institutionalised bullying. He bravely went for his cello tuition and was put in detention for pursuing with dedication a gift that some felt you had given him.

Did you look down on him the day he spent his lunchtime cleaning his classmate's rugby boots as punishment for missing sports to attend a cello lesson and observe how he suffered for his art? He developed a steely determination to counter injustice. He read Steve Biko's biography *Cry Freedom* and understood the premise that egalitarianism was worth fighting for. His compassion and idealism turned him into a feisty character prepared to stand up to authority and air his views. He reminds me of how I used to be, before I allowed myself to slot into the conventional lifestyle dictated by my upbringing.

The Love of Music

I took James to concerts and recitals and relished the time we spent together. He rekindled my love of music and through his eyes I rediscovered a part of me that had lain dormant for so long. Before he went to Chethams, we had heard the world's finest cellists perform at the Royal Northern College of Music in Manchester during the International Cello Festival. I had no inkling then that a few years later I would hear my son play the cello in this prestigious venue as a member of Chetham's orchestra performing Vaughan Williams haunting 'Variations on a Theme by Thomas Tallis'.

James' cello teacher had ceased to be peripatetic. Once a week I collected James from school and travelled to his teacher's home, 50 miles away. Tom stayed at school and had tea with the boarders and we picked him up on the way home. On cold winter nights I drove home in the dark down the A1 with James asleep in the passenger seat. This balancing act was becoming increasingly difficult. Was John Allen your envoy, popping up with a solution when I didn't even realise I was seeking one? The seed was sown and I broached the subject of Chetham's school with James' cello teacher, who recoiled with horror at the suggestion. She was eager to hold on to her pupil. She protested that there was so much more she could teach him but we needed to see what this "special school" could offer him. The pride I felt in the knowledge that James possessed the "Chetham's Spark" was tinged with sadness. I was going to lose his close companionship but during his long absences from home I was finally able to give my undivided attention to Tom. He missed James as much as I did but as always accepted the status quo. I conquered my fear of driving on the motorway and in complex one-way systems in unfamiliar cities to journey as frequently as I could, and as was appropriate, to Manchester.

At this unique school James was afforded every assistance in all subjects. He coped well with the rigorous demands of four hours music tuition and practice each day and continued to work hard at the other subjects that were so important to him. His biology teacher nurtured his passion for zoology and became a mentor and friend to James during the difficult settling in period. Sports were not on the curriculum, hardly surprising considering the nature of the school, and James missed playing rugby and cricket especially but kept fit using the school's swimming pool, gym and squash courts. He made friends from all corners of the globe and from disparate backgrounds, and some of these friendships continue to stand the test of time.

Although he went on to study zoology at Manchester University, James kept his links with musician friends who went on to study at the Royal Northern College of Music and he continued to play in a quartet. Through music he met the girl who was to become his wife. She had come from Seattle in the States to study at the Royal Northern College of Music. When James and Julia graduated she flew back to Seattle and after some months he followed her. In a quirky ceremony beside a totem pole next to a lake he married his Julia, who sings with Seattle Opera. James is now a cancer research scientist at the prestigious Fred Hutchinson Cancer Research Department at the University of Washington in Seattle.

Tom's Talipes

James' "Special Education" led to a life we would never have envisaged for him. Whilst this fascinating life was developing for James in Manchester, Tom continued to enjoy and benefit from the nurturing environment at his special school. Life was interrupted periodically for medical intervention, mainly for his Talipes but there were also visits to the orthoptist and eye specialist who diagnosed astigmatism. On the occasions when Tom fell or tripped the assumption had been that the cause was his clubfoot and cerebral palsy; it seemed his poor eyesight had contributed to the problem.

Tom's foot had reached a stage where the foot and leg had developed sufficiently for what would hopefully be the final operation. Would this give Tom a foot that worked, a foot that would keep a boot on for more than a few shuffling steps? Tom's orthopaedic surgeon didn't pull his punches. He informed us that the wedge osteoctomy was a hideous operation. A wedge of bone would be removed from the top of the foot and the two surfaces of bone would be pushed together and stapled. Tom's leg would then be encased in a plaster cast from toe to thigh. Tom would be in terrible pain when he came round from the operation and this would last for some time afterwards. His pain was alleviated by morphine, which he was given via injection for several days. After Tom came back from theatre, I lived and slept beside his bed in a crowded and busy children's ward for some days. After he came round from the anaesthetic, the surgeon visited. All had gone well, he said, but on no account should Tom be allowed to attempt to get out of bed and put weight on his foot. Tom was ashen and the plaster cast stained with blood caused by seepage from the operation. In this awful condition he managed a typical genial Tom comment: “It's a nice place this, I'm fine”.

Far From Fine

He was far from fine but didn't complain. He needed constant supervision and nursing. The children's ward was a familiar environment to us both. Tom had progressed from the baby cubicles and cots through to the top end of the ward with other teenagers. Things had changed a great deal from Sister Williams' day. She had been efficient and caring, with her reassuring manner and wealth of experience gleaned during a long nursing career, and she was a source of knowledge and expertise for junior doctors, patients and mothers. But the Sister Williams of the NHS had been usurped by a more economical system that relied on agency nurses who could not and did not know their patients as people. I longed for Sister Williams' reassurance and the comforting cups of tea she would appear with when the going got rough.

I barely left the bedside, so anxious was I when Tom was left alone. Once I returned from the loo to find him covered in blood from a severe nosebleed. No one had noticed and he was attempting to mop up the mess with tissues. Another time I discovered he had attempted to get out of bed to reach a ‘bottle’ so he could have a pee. He was soaked with urine and embarrassed. I berated the nurse I had asked to keep an eye on him. As soon as he started to recover and make progress I discharged him from the ward. The post-op. nursing was inadequate and I could nurse him better at home. The ward manager was, to say the least, annoyed. I received no assistance transferring my son from bed to wheelchair and departing from the ward. I needed every ounce of strength I could muster to hoist him from wheelchair into the passenger seat of my car. I've never been so happy to get home. Despite all we would have to cope with over the next few months I knew I'd made the right decision.

As soon as he was able, Tom returned to Welburn Hall in pot leg and wheelchair, where the complications of visits to the loo, transfers between lessons and activities were handled brilliantly by the care staff. Tom was cheerful and patient but I was exhausted. For example, bathing my hefty teenage son needed strength and ingenuity. First, I wrapped the pot leg in supermarket carriers. Then I climbed into the bath, semi-naked, and stood behind Tom with my arms under his. A count of three prepared us for our huge effort and whilst Phil held the pot leg out of the water, we would heave him in. It was equally hard hoisting him out and I suppose no surprise that on one occasion a searing pain shot through my back and Tom and I collapsed in a heap on the bathroom floor. The pain from the squeezed disc was excruciating. For the next six months I also had to fit in travelling, with great difficulty, fifteen miles to the local hospital for regular physiotherapy. Looking back, it amazes me how we coped. The support of Welburn Hall School was terrific and I'm sure that is what kept me going.

Leaving Welburn

All too soon, though, Tom's Welburn years drew to a close. Reviews took place annually. The last Welburn Hall review was held as Tom was approaching his 16th birthday. We joined the assembled group of professionals to discuss his future. For 12 years Welburn's care staff, therapists and teachers had given me peace of mind whilst Tom was in their charge. He was secure in this environment, and here lay the problem. If Tom moved on to Welburn's Independence Unit, it was felt he could become too dependent on the secure world he lived in.

Although this was not what I wanted for Tom, I went along with their decision. We began to search for a college Tom would enjoy and flourish in. This was not to be an easy task. Number one on the list as far as Tom was concerned was the opportunity to work with animals. It seemed we had found the perfect place when we visited a Steiner college in idyllic grounds with pigs, sheep, chickens and a dairy herd. But the Steiner ethos does not suit everyone. Although there would be animals, Steiner promotes a self-contained community lifestyle, which Tom would have found hard to adjust to. Tom is a sociable individual, he loves to watch television and his videos, especially animated ones, he enjoys trips to the pub for a game of pool and a pint or two of beer and he regularly makes trips to the cinema. He would no longer have been able to enjoy any of these activities on a regular basis.

We finally settled on Dilston Mencap College, over a hundred miles away. For me there was no peace of mind. This was made worse by the lack of communication from the college. Between visits I was in perpetual anguish about Tom's well being. My fears were not unfounded. One of the worst incidents was when an autistic pupil assaulted Tom. The two had been sent over a main road together as part of a road safety exercise. The staff member in charge had failed to observe their progress and when he did look round, Tom was lying at the edge of the road with the other pupil on top of him scratching his face. This incident warranted an official report. My shock and anger was not allayed when social services informed me that "These things happen in these institutions". I retorted that it had never happened to my gentle, vulnerable son during the twelve years that he had been a pupil at Welburn Hall School.

No Peace of Mind

There were other incidents that caused me enormous concern. These feelings were compounded when James' visit home coincided with Dilston College's garden party. James was shocked by Tom's dishevelled appearance. He had withdrawn into himself and picked up mannerisms from fellow students in the unit he'd recently been placed in. There had been no consultation with us about Tom's move from the cottage he shared with students with similar abilities to himself to a unit with pupils who had even more severe learning difficulties. After putting pen to paper and voicing our concerns with the college and social services, Tom was moved to another unit, Chapel Cottage, with more able pupils and after some initial settling in problems the situation improved dramatically.

A new Key Worker gave me confidence that Tom would benefit from the move and the support she gave him was excellent. Communication with her was good. In Tom's final year, despite Key Worker changes, he benefited from the companionship of his friends in the cottage and from the many challenges, including Outward Bound expeditions, which he probably would not otherwise have experienced.

On balance, and despite the genuine helpfulness of many staff, I find it difficult to decide whether the good that came out of Tom's three years at Mencap College were worth the trauma. I am grateful, though, for Tom's last Key Worker, Jo. She gave valuable advice and co-operation in the next transition period we underwent. She travelled with Tom to meet us and help in an assessment of a college recommended to us by social services.

Well, God, we drifted apart here, didn't we? During Tom and James' school years and their transition to manhood, I barely spoke to you. Occasionally I would visit York Minster to pray and light a candle for James and Julia when they were about to travel between Seattle and England. I thought about you when I thought about those who had gone the extra mile for us, whether prompted by Christian beliefs or an extraordinary humanity. They had made a difference. They sustained me and gave me hope for the future when life was grim and challenging.

The Next Phase

Now Tom and I are moving into another phase in our lives. He's been home for two years now but this spring he moved into Sutton Cottage with four other young men with disabilities. The Wilf Ward Trust manages the house and in this supported accommodation he will have a home for life. Tom is ecstatic. He'll have a degree of independence I would not have thought possible ten years ago. It will be hard to adjust to being me again. After all, for twenty years I've been Tom's mum and carer but now I intend to live life to the full. The excitement of what lies ahead lifts my spirits. I don't look back to who or what I might have been because the experience of being a mother to my two special sons has changed me so profoundly. I'm 55; I don't need to conform to any image any longer. I'm going to enjoy my freedom, learn to love myself and discover those things I've been afraid to embark upon before and, God, I shall try to re-establish my relationship with you. If I've berated you for not being there for me during the last twenty years, I apologise unreservedly. It's only with hindsight we see the complete picture. There was no loud booming voice but you did speak to me, didn't you?

You spoke clearly, if somewhat belatedly, on a cold, wet, autumn day in Manchester in 2002. Tom and I were collecting James from his student accommodation. Rusholme is a poor run down area. Its largely immigrant population sits alongside students who are just passing through, waiting for opportunity to beckon them on to cleaner, brighter streets. You spoke to me there, quietly. On this greyest of days in these grubby terraced streets a spectral image appeared to me. You were showing me something I will remember until the day I die. As I stepped from my car, a man lurched towards the edge of the pavement in front of me. I recognised his characteristic club foot gait but the degree of his deformity was shocking. The foot was in a black laced boot with a deep built-up platform. It was twisted so badly that walking just a few yards must have been tortuous. His arm in spasm betrayed his cerebral palsy. He shuffled across the road, his huge Oxfam grey coat flapping around him, and disappeared into the gloomy mist.

He was what my son should have become, would have become, without intervention, divine or otherwise.
I can see that now. I see why we had to endure the unendurable all those years.

Libby Fletcher

My Daughter

Writing about my daughter's disability and how she copes in our physical world could fill the pages of a book, but that way you would never get to know her. I prefer to write about her abilities, her dreams, her aspirations. Her spirit never fails to amaze me.

I have written for hours, months, years about my daughter's trials and tribulations. About the difficulties experienced from birth, the extensive surgery, the mountains we have climbed. It tells you nothing about who she is.

What can I tell you about my daughter? She loves life. She loves herself. She is the most positive person I have ever met. She is a typical teenager, wilful, amazing. She sees life from a different angle (which is good, this enhances my viewpoint) she loves shopping, socialising, music, soaps, reality TV shows, her dog. She loves her wheelchair, her friends and more shopping. Having her and my other children in my life has been and continues to be the most positive life changing experience imaginable. I used to get depressed by the nothingness of life. She brings a positive attitude towards everything into our lives, something for which I shall be eternally grateful.

A Mum

Taking Care

Spring again. At this time of year women's magazines are full of articles titled 'Spring clean your life', 'De-clutter and energise yourself'. Then suddenly among the exhortations to streamline your wardrobe and toss out your collection of pottery pigs you will also be urged to throw away 'people who are keeping you stuck and stopping you from moving on'. Out they go – miserable Granny with her arthritis, the fat asthmatic spaniel and that untidy child in the wheelchair. Now – don't you feel better?

The aspirations these magazines express don't sit very comfortably with the reality facing me. I sometimes amuse myself composing lifestyle features for people like me – "100 ways you can have fun with a stair-lift", "Make a design statement with your bath aid". I don't think I'll get very far. Wheelchair and chic are not words that go together.

There is a powerful myth that successful women these days can have it all – a career, a wonderful marriage with very presentable husband, perfect children and a perfect figure. Their families are run along the lines of efficient and highly productive industries and childcare is timetabled with military precision. Now as central government intrudes ever deeper into our private affairs, with parenting education projects and the like, can it be long before we start having performance indicators for parents, parental outputs and family outcomes, to satisfy our masters in Whitehall? Successful families would qualify for bonuses, while idlers could have their child benefit docked.

The Ranks of Nice People

This emphasis on measurability in what should be a private sphere may lie behind the jargon term parent-carer. I frequently receive correspondence addressed to "Parent-carer" and I am always irritated by this label. Invariably I ask myself what it means – am I a parent *or* a carer or am I a parent *and* a carer? Are not all parents carers, or only those of us with disabled children? Does being a parent-carer set me apart? Hal is special, I am a parentcarer. Then I chastise myself, ahh don't be so bitter and twisted – parentcarer sounds *nice*. At last, I have joined the ranks of nice people: I am a carer.

A quick glance at the dictionary upsets the warm runny feeling that has begun to envelop me. To 'care' has meanings including 'to sorrow', 'to be troubled' as well as 'to look after'. In Shakespeare's *King Henry the Fourth* the King is 'shaken...wan with care'. I too begin to feel wan, as ever more envelopes addressed to that hybrid monster, the parentcarer, drop on my doormat.

Perhaps I am supposed to be pleased with the appellation, un-euphonious though it is. It is intended to acknowledge my special role. I am someone. A carer, recognised and taken into account. A carer – just one letter from career, but with rather fewer financial compensations. There might be some value in being a carer if it was worth my while. Well of course there is Carer's Allowance: in March 2006 £45.70 a week provided I don't get a part-time job. If I do and if I then earn a penny over £82 a week, I will lose the whole amount. The caring responsibilities will remain however. Carer's allowance is also counted as taxable income.

Forget the Freebies

The term (and the generous benefit) deceives the envious who imagine that as a carer I qualify for all kinds of freebies. And the term introduces further conflict when you are divorced from your child's father as I am. Hal's father A. and I separated when Hal was three years old. At first I imagined that care of both boys would be shared equally between us. Then various incidents began to cast their shadow over my admittedly idealistic vision, and I realised that many different forces govern what happens to relations between parents and children after divorce.

One time sticks in my mind. It was Hal's fourth birthday, a Saturday, and I had asked A. to bring Hal home at lunchtime so that I would be able to see him on his special day. Hal was returned, but by his grandfather. This was the first clue I had that for several months, when I had been led to believe that Hal was spending time with his father, he had in fact been taken to his grandparents' house. T. my other son was spending the weekends with A. and his girlfriend of the moment. It turned out that the girlfriend was not too keen on having a handicapped child around. Then, as now, Hal had no speech, but over the months when this had been going on, and I was kept in the dark, I had noticed an increase in his seizures and a tendency to be more withdrawn than usual, though A. refused point blank to believe that Hal's fits had anything to do with his care (or lack of it). It was at about this time that A. suggested that it would be fairer if T. came to live with him permanently. He would leave Hal with me. In the course of time the girlfriend left him – to marry someone with "fewer personal problems" – and A. now feeling rather lonely, started looking after both boys again. Hal immediately became calmer and happier. Like any other child he loves his father.

With the arrival of a new girlfriend, contact with Hal once again became the focus of conflict. A. refused to see Hal except at specific times, decided by him without discussion or negotiation, times when he need never pay for childcare, or be inconvenienced by the conflict of family and work commitments which are a fact of life for everyone with children or a family.

Choosing to Care

He tried to justify his position by saying that I am Hal's carer and "receive all the corresponding benefits". He has always maintained that I owe him a proportion of Hal's disability living allowance and child benefit, in spite of the fact that he abandoned both children for more than a year, and used the time to settle himself in a lucrative career, and that he has a household income four times mine. The combination of my 'carer' and 'parent with residence' labels seem to have persuaded him that he has no real responsibility or obligations.

He doesn't accept, or perhaps even recognise, that I have, for the time being, given up the chance of a serious career, and that this was not in any real sense a choice. His choice, to walk away from the problem, meant that I had no choice of my own. My only choice was to respond to his choice. I decided to face the consequences of the situation, not to turn tail and run, however tempting that might have seemed. I chose to grasp the difficulty, and attempt to redeem it, trying to do it well, and with grace.

And at some level, I seem to have become an object of envy to A. He desperately wants equal recognition as Hal's carer, despite the fact that his main priority has been to make sure his life is distanced from the ups and downs and stays comfortable, secure and predictable. Only then is he available to offer (limited) help with Hal. Ah well, perhaps he is right. Maybe I too should have refused to care for my son until I had established myself in a career, bought a house, sorted out my relationship. Flying by the seat of your pants as I do is hardly ideal. The trouble was that Hal just kept being there, needing feeding, changing, bathing, entertaining, helping to grow. I couldn't just switch him off until a more convenient moment because with real live children the show must go on.

Gillian Upton Holmes

The Art of Parenting

Tough. No doubt about that. None at all.
Hold your breath. Count to ten. A hundred. A thousand. Then breathe.
Everything you know has been overturned. Overnight. Keep breathing.
At times it feels too much, too fast, too soon. But there is amazing joy.
Really. And enjoyment you never knew possible in tiny simple things.
Treasure them. And nurture respect. Respect for yourself, for your child.
Okay: there'll be gossip, condescension, pity, the downright objectionable.
Fuck them, we say. You're the oasis maker, trouble taker. You keep breathing.
Put your child at the world's centre: at the still point of your churning heart.
And you work and toil and toil and work, labouring to keep them there.
Remember that it can be fun a lot of the time.
Even when grandma says: "Nice children don't do that." Keep breathing.
Nothing compares to this love affair.
Tiny little star shaped hands: I hold you to my heart, little one.
I'll fight for you forever. You keep breathing.
Never say never. Never pretend it should have been different..
Go out into that wide, wondering world.
Breathe.
Keep breathing.
Take me with you.

Rebecca O'Rourke

4 Picture This

This collection of photographs comes from our family albums. They are just like your family photos: some of them are out of focus, some of them are embarrassing, some of them are very unflattering; but we treasure them. It can be embarrassing to come across photos like these in publications such as ours. They are not professional, they can be a bit blurry and you don't know the people or the context. So, why are they here?

We think it is important that they are here because they tell part of the story. They show us living lives that are sometimes extraordinary, because the experience is one that few people will share, but most of the time our lives are just like anybody else's. We are proud to share these images of our children: we want to put them, and you, in the picture.

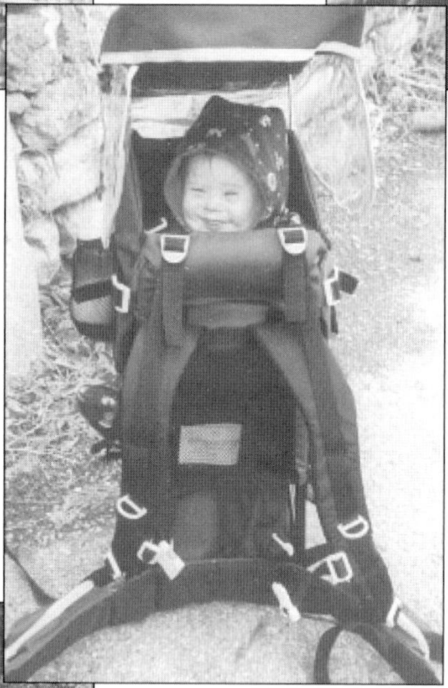

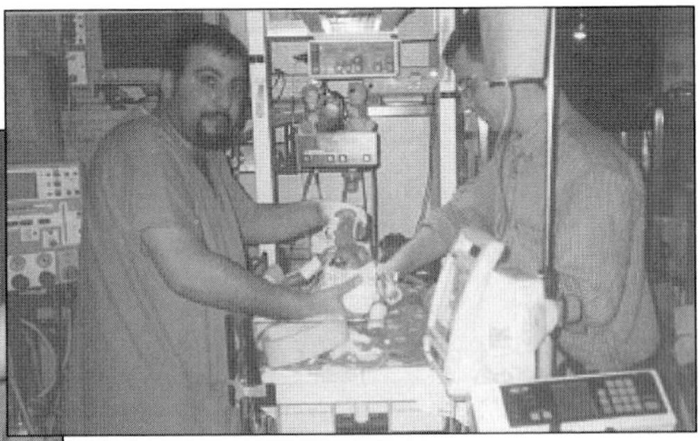

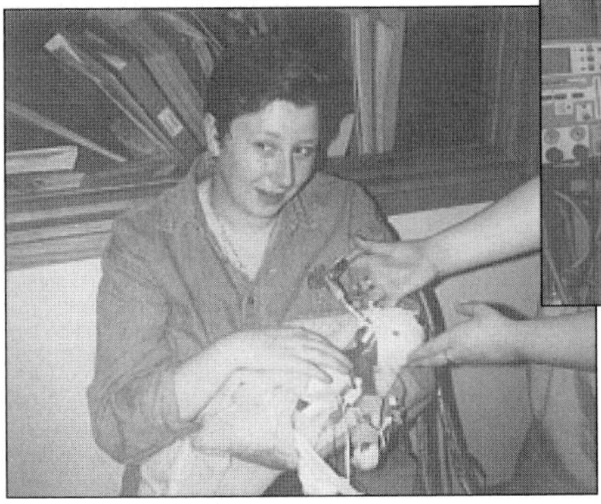

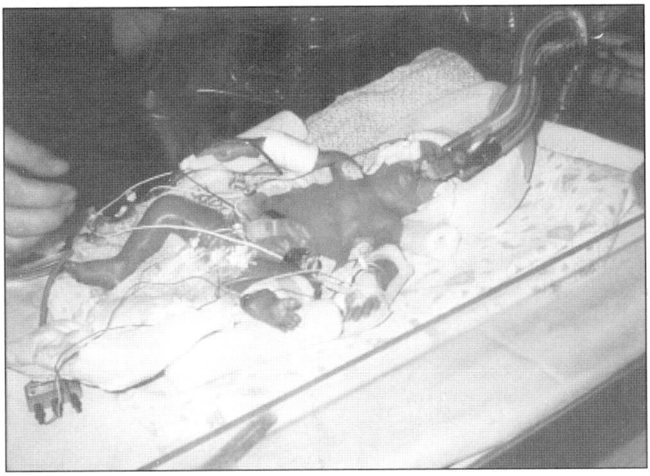

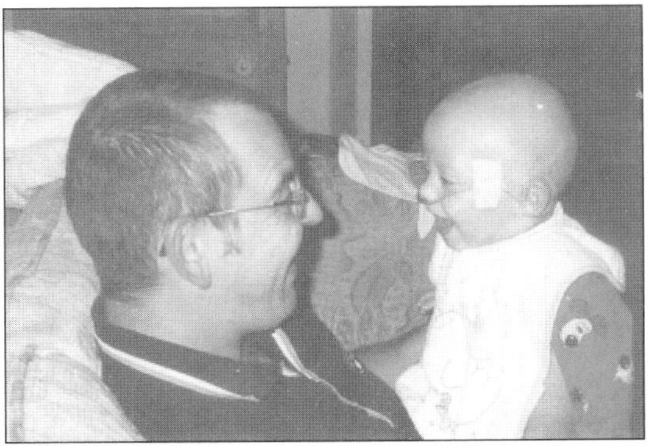

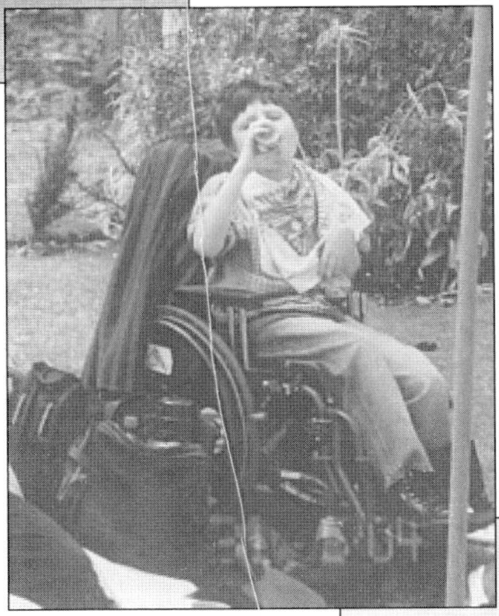

CAUTION

Reflections

When you look at me
Who do you see?
Do you see the same as me?
Or a reflection of yourself
Projected and unconsciously placed in me?
Do you draw from me
What you need to see
In order to maintain
Your expected view of reality?

A Mum

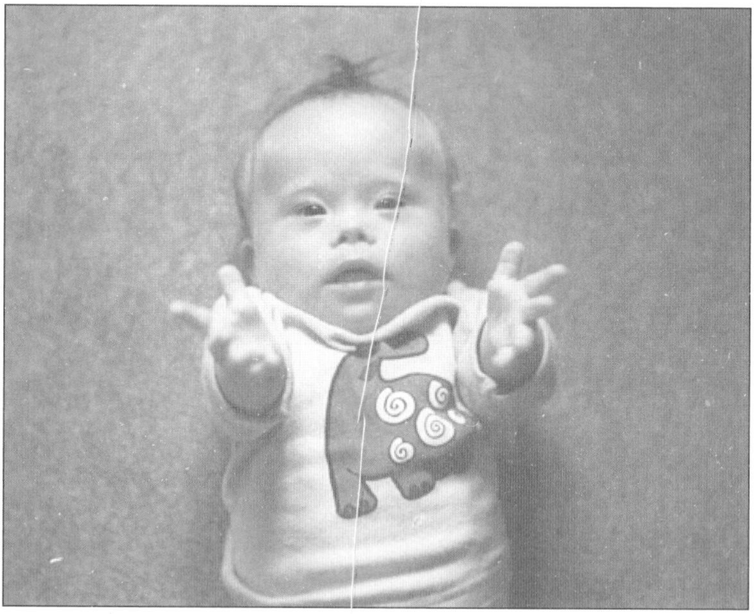

5 Disability PLC

The professionals

Many parents marvel at the sheer number of experts deemed necessary to their child's well-being.

The professionals, that brigade of experts who march into your life, often into your house, where they drink all your coffee, tell you a hundred things you don't want to know or alternatively keep everything totally secret with the tenacity of a member of the French Resistance under torture.

There's a paediatrician for the whole child and a consultant paediatrician for all the bits where something is wrong. Hal had experts for eyes (5), ears (2 and a nurse) and teeth (2). He had a speech therapist – they are not only for speech (which he can't do), but also for language and communication, and swallowing as well. That's thirteen already and we're only down to the neck.

Hal had an occupational therapist for adapting things he holds, sits, stands or lies on, and a physiotherapist as well, who stretches him out, stands him up and issues boots and splints. Then there are splint specialists (latex or rigid, sir?) and a neurologist for botox injections to loosen stiff muscles. Wheelchairs are assessed and issued by a wheelchair specialist, who is also a physiotherapist, but not the same one as for seats and stretching. Swimming was sometimes done by physios, and sometimes by volunteers, but mostly it was not done at all which was a pity, as it is the one thing which is both good for him and enjoyable. In the case of a specific problem, say epilepsy as in Hal's case, there's an expert for that too. And before a child starts school you may also be in touch with an Educational Psychologist, a pre-school teacher, a pre-school setting SENCO (Special Educational Needs Co-ordinator), a Portage worker and a Parent Partnership officer.

FACT: By the time a disabled child reaches the age of 5, he (and his dazed and confused mama) will have seen an average of 33 different professionals

At five, Education became the Lead Agency, which from my point of view meant that no one came to my house any more, because it was easier to see my child at school. I saved a fortune in coffee, but started to feel a little out of touch with what was going on with all the therapists. Their roles blurred into one, and when they phoned or wrote notes in his child's home schoolbook, I would often bluster helplessly as I failed to remember who they were. It was a bit like being an amnesiac at a cocktail party.

The Social Worker soon made inroads into my coffee again however. Social workers must fill in lengthy assessment forms which take hours to complete. A young social worker once tried to arrange four three-hour interviews with me. When I had stopped laughing, I declined his offer, and suggested that he make up as much as he could on his own and just check any details with me (presumably he needed to know our genealogical details since the battle of Waterloo, the makes of car driven by my maternal grandfather and which side my father parted his hair and other facts only I would know), but sadly he left the job a few weeks later – a pity, his assessment would, with the amount of research he was proposing, have been the length of an average Victorian novel.

So far I have mentioned only a few of the experts you get on the NHS. What about the alternatives? Entering the waters of alternative therapies can be a challenge as these are shark-infested seas. *"Shark Cartilage – a new cure for brain-damage, cancer etc. Also guaranteed to make you win the lottery!!!"* But it isn't just the literal sharks that are worrying; of the million wonder cures out there from homeopathy to Snake Oil via Brushing and Cranial Osteopathy, how do you begin to choose one that might be useful? I've often wondered if my time might be used better if I forgot about it all, and chose a real alternative like spending the money on a bottle of wine and a pizza.

Some more enlightened policy makers have realised that all these experts, all carrying out separate assessments, and turning the mildest of parents into ranting, carpet-chewing revolutionaries, may not be the ideal solution. Care co-ordination is the remarkable notion that basic information about a child could be collected once and shared among the relevant professionals on a need to know basis. The Care co-ordinator responsible for this would be chosen by the family from among the hordes of people they already see. Now wouldn't that be marvellous? Maybe some tunnels really do have light at the end of them.

Gillian Upton Holmes

Us

They let me take you to my room, David. Past the beige walls and faded noticeboards along the warm airless corridor on institutional brown nylon carpet from the Special Care Baby Unit. Away from the security, the entry buzzer, the over bright lights, the awe-inspiring machinery, the quiet subdued parents, busy but bored nurses and tiny, tiny skinned-rabbit babies in glossy incubators and plastic fish tank cots.

You had your little security tag removed from your skinny ankle but you still had your naso-gastric tube and were connected to a huge black leaden oxygen cylinder. You weren't quite mine to pick up freely, to whirl around and dance and play with (we'd make up for that later, little one!). So, I was cautious not to yank your tubes, your security, your life, your umbilical cord connecting you to the hospital and not to me.

I carefully positioned myself and sat you on my lap, in an easy chair – still institutionalised with its hardwearing fabric and wooden arms. I nuzzled your head and face and smelt your musty baby hair. I stroked your little floppy arms, skin soft and new and smooth, unravaged, your tiny star shaped hands and pointy sharp fingernails.

I didn't know what to do with a baby, my baby. I picked up the nearest thing to hand, the Radio Times, and showed you the pages. Bright red pages, adverts, gashes and splashes of colour. Your eyes opened so wide, so big, in awe, so amazed. You took it all in, my bright and beautiful clever boy.

I considered what to do next, not natural yet, this. No nurse to ask, no routine to follow. Evening, quietening, darkness, subdued, winding down, warm, tired, I carefully lifted you onto the bed, tubes trailing, and laid you on your side. You're still now, passive, accepting, sleepy. I wrapped you in a blanket – white and starchy, standard issue acrylic cellular. Taking care with your fragile tubes, I lay with you and held you carefully, utterly private now, no one else. No other parents or grandparents unable to resist peeping, glancing, asking, adding interest to their Sunday afternoon out. No nurses asking briskly, ticking boxes, whether your last nappy was wet

Just me, holding you. Me: tentative, cautious, in new territory, reaching out, exploring. You: trusting, accepting; just being a baby. Tiny stirrings of Mumminess, of Us.

Sue Smith

The Ideal Mother

I often wonder where I went wrong.

Why didn't I realise that all mothers of disabled children are brave little martyrs who don't expect to have jobs, or social lives? They accept with cow-like docility the contradictory advice from a range of experts. They don't argue and they never, ever, ever, get cross.

Resourceful and gifted handywomen, they are good at everything from adapting a highchair so a stiff-legged three-year-old can sit in it, to mending a wheelchair that has collapsed in the middle of a Spanish airport.

Unlike other women of their generation, they always expected to stay at home with their children, they like nothing better than working through the lists of painful and tedious activities handed to them by physiotherapists, speech therapists, every otherpists and none of this frustrates them at all.

They are in fact a kind of Stepford Mother, designed entirely for the comfort and convenience of the professionals who deal with their children.

Why don't hospitals hand out uniforms at diagnosis? How about flowery pinnies, sensible shoes and a 1950s hairdo?

Required reading for the Ideal Mother are 'inspirational' books with titles like *Brain Damage, what Brain Damage?* whose regimes would need a degree of mania to attempt.

But even the routines devised by physios, O.T.s and speech therapists for newly diagnosed children, if carried out by anyone other than the Ideal Mother, would amount to a Stakhanovite regime, with precious little time to waste on washing one's own hair or reading the paper, let alone my preferred pleasures of drinking gin and reading for longer than five minutes a week.

Little wonder that among the families of disabled children, marriages collapse at an alarming rate, 84 per cent of mothers do no paid work at all, and that all these demands induce Catholic levels of guilt in even the most robust of parents.

Of course we want to give our children the best chance we can, but it is easy to become infected by the mood of professionals caught up in the need to fix our children, make them better by doing something significant.

I believe the task of parenting is different, slower, more relaxed and imaginative than the charts and the routines which so many professionals wave in front of us. Intuitive, gentle, more art than science, and, just as in the best-lived lives, there are no hard and fast rules about the best way to be a parent of any child, whoever they are and whatever their abilities.

Gillian Upton Holmes

Lost

Three and a half months in Scarborough Hospital, three and a half months of mapping out this new life and this tiny little world of the tiny frail baby, the well trodden corridor to the Special Care Baby Unit and to your room. The mealtimes, the food, the shift pattern, the nurses. Three and a half months of the unfamiliar territory becoming totally and utterly familiar, your new life, your old life receding into the distance and far away. Three and a half months of waiting for him to put on enough weight to be ready for his heart operation in Leeds, yearning for a date, asking the Doctor every morning on the rounds "Have you heard from Leeds yet?" Striving for that day, everything, all our strength and will focussed on that day – on just getting there.

Where's the Map?

The day comes and you fall apart. You just can't cope and the tears flow and flow. You are in a totally new, much slicker, much bigger regional children's heart surgery ward in Leeds General Infirmary. You are totally disorientated and overwhelmed. You've had the official tour now and you've never felt so lost. Why don't they provide a map? All the new faces. So many names, titles and routines to assimilate. Who are the friendly faces? Who will understand? You desperately want to keep on breast feeding David, and to supply milk for his tube feeds. But there's a new breast pump and you've no idea how it works, or who to ask. You long for the ancient but familiar machine back in Scarborough. And you suddenly realise you are desperately, desperately homesick, homesick for a hospital that became your home.

Homesick for the familiar nurses, even the crabby ones, for the curtains with owls on, for the milk kitchen, for the other babies, for the corridors so frequently trod, for the shift pattern now hardwired into your brain, for time that seems never ending, for the enveloping security, so cosy and warm. And now there's a seismic shift and you find yourself standing on a precipice, staring into the jaws of David's heart operation – and then what? Of course you knew you couldn't stay in Scarborough Hospital forever, and in the beginning you never knew or imagined it would be this long, but now ... But now it's become your life, wrapped itself around you, more real than reality.

And of course you are continually telling everyone brightly that "Ooh yes, you just can't wait to get him home, home at last, to be a proper family". But inside, deep inside, you know that actually you'd quite like to always be this safe and looked after, just you and your baby, for a lot, lot longer.

The tears start to flow, and an unknown nurse comes to see what's the matter. She assumes it is because the surgeon has just been to explain tomorrow's procedure and get your signature on the consent form. How can you explain that it's not that? That David is in their hands, you trust them to just get on with it and do it. It's just that you feel so lost, confused and homesick? You are feeling slightly ashamed of such childlike behaviour – knowing you should be the responsible, strong, devoted, earnest parent willing her baby on. But you just feel lost and want a mummy yourself. It feels like a play, a game of make believe, of doctors and nurses, with dollies.

Finding A Way

Next morning David is in a cot with a tiny, tiny surgery gown on, on top of his nappy. It looks like pretend, you didn't know they made them that small, or that they were necessary. He looks so innocent and cute and smiles his morning smile, once again. You and John carry him, cuddle him, with the team to the operating theatre. Then you have to say bye-bye, to hand him over and let them do what they have to do to his little walnut sized heart. You are reassured he is in safe hands, they cuddle him too, he looks happy and interested, anticipating his next adventure.

And what do you do now? What is expected? What is your role? You cannot, simply cannot, sit around waiting for five hours or more, others could; you can't. You find yourself in Leeds, shopping, HMV and Body Shop have sales still and you are enjoying buying some bargains. Only occasionally do you remember the desperately, desperately significant and momentous events continuing up the hill at the hospital and you can't believe you are here, doing this, studying exfoliating soaps and tea tree shampoo. You are still experiencing a detachment, feel cut adrift from reality, from home, from yourself. Strange and weird. Right now, you have no responsibility. There is *nothing* you can do, it really is out of your hands and it's really quite a relief. You may be a terrible parent right now but dithering over cosmetics won't *actually* make any difference to what is happening. And later, you see him in intensive care and *everything* is being done for him. He is fed with a tube, he wees into a tube, the machines have taken over the responsibility now. Watch and wait, from a distance. The hours and days unfold, he comes round, he moves from intensive care to high dependency to normal ward. You begin to find your way around, to find your place again, as David's Mum. You are astonished at how well he can feed now without becoming breathless, and you find you have your new and improved baby back. He has a big scar on his chest, but it heals well and you are dressing him and changing him once again.

Coming Home

When we eventually came home, I was ready. Terrified but ready, even though, in the end, it happened so suddenly. We were taken back to Scarborough but to the children's ward, not the womb-like Special Care Baby Unit that I had been so homesick for a week ago. I slept in a room *with* David. I got up in the night to feed him when he cried. I was summoned naturally by his cry, not by an intercom buzzer from the nurse on night shift. On Sunday morning a doctor checks him over and says he thinks we can go home now. And when I say "Now?" He says "Now – This afternoon"!

John is astonished when he turns up to visit as normal, never dreaming this will be the last time. And it's hard to recollect exactly. He came home this time, not for an afternoon's visit, with no oxygen cylinders or tubes – just a baby. We are told he still needs to put on weight, so I should set my alarm to get up and feed him every four hours at night. Somehow we just get on with it, and time lets our new life together unfold naturally. At first we are buffered with the health visitor's visits and the kindness, love and presents of friends coming to welcome him. It's lovely and the landscape of my life begins to come back into focus, confidence in myself returns and I welcome again the freedom of the responsibility of being grown up. We can eat *when* we want, what we want, go out for long walks with the pram, and sod it if he wants feeding when there is something good on telly. In Special Care Baby Unit I was dragged away from my room by the intercom; now I just grab him and settle down again. Feet up, glass of wine nearby. Early mornings he just snuggles into bed with us – no need to make myself half-decent before trudging the corridor for that early morning feed.

And I'm able to cope with the chest infections that mean a regular short stay in Scarborough Hospital Children's Ward. I take it in my stride. His immune system is not quite able to fight off colds yet, surely it will be one day. The nurses there get to know us and adore

David. Once, as we wheeled him in, he grinned and blew a huge raspberry – his usual greeting, as if to say "Hi it's me. I'm back". And I'm able to cope with the regular cardiac check ups. The verdict is that his surgery has been very successful and I'm very proud.

Then on the way to our first summer holiday together in Norfolk, we stop at Grandma and Grandad's in Sheffield. David's poorly again and Grandma's worried. She calls the doctor and he's admitted to Sheffield Children's Hospital. Once again I feel small and lost and bewildered in another huge unknown hospital. He does recover this time but the world shifts on its axis as a Sheffield consultant suggests bluntly that each successive chest infection may be putting a little more strain on his heart and it may be that sooner or later he will not recover. I'm cut adrift again, away from the familiar territory of our life together and there is no comfort, no way home. In fact there is no home. There is only the temporary shelter of raised hopes and reassurance along the way, but the end of our journey is inevitable. Three months later little David dies aged 13 months, in Leeds, and the map is finally ripped up.

Sue Smith

Suffer

Suffer
Suffer little children
I saw that
Please breathe

Breathe
Breath of life
I drew breath
And watched your pain

Pain
Pain for days
And when it eased
Hurt clawed through me

Me
Me your mother
You called for me
I wasn't there

There
There for you
To succour you
When hope left home

Home
Home is where the heart is
A heart that pounds
When bone is sawn

Sawn
Sawn grief soaked
Grieving for ever
Drowning in grey

Grey
Grey the colour of your bed
Bed that rocks
Rocks you now

Now
Now here with me
Arms like vices
Hold you tight

Tight
Tight into the night
Daytime's demons
Battled out.

Libby Fletcher

6 Schooling, Prejudice and Politics

Inclusive Education Part 1 – "The Parent"

As baby David's Mum I was so proud of all his achievements, his new skills and interactions with others. I rejoiced to hear professionals comment favourably on his intellectual progress, alertness and interest. My heart soared at the stories of how he was frequently grabbed from his childminder at the toddler group and carried off into the staff room of the little Catholic school where the group was held. Carried off to be fussed, cuddled and passed around. To clap and smile and giggle and perform for the staff's delight. I was overjoyed when Fiona, his childminder, told me that the head teacher at St Joseph's wanted David to come to her school and was hoping Fiona would be able to persuade me. *Persuade* me? I would have *loved* to see him go there.

John and I had read and heard a lot about the issues surrounding educational provision for children with special needs in the few months since David was born. We knew about hurdles of assessments, statements, bureaucracy ahead but now we felt that with a head teacher willing to welcome him our pathway might be a little easier. We began to look to the future. We imagined him in a little royal blue sweatshirt and grey trousers, running round the playground with his new friends and peers. Young and innocent, all of them, not yet polluted by peer pressure and prejudice, intellectual differences not yet glaring. John wanted to volunteer to take a little football team to help the school, to show our gratitude. We didn't think much further ahead, didn't dare yet. This was enough for now. We would cross the secondary school bridge when we came to it ... Who knew how different things would be in a decade's time, given the rate at which things were changing?

Inclusive Education Part 2: "The Teacher"

As a secondary school teacher my heart sank when, on the first training day back in September an extra staff meeting was slotted in. We were all to assemble in the hall, to hear important information about the children with special needs in this year's new intake. But this meeting's coming out of my precious preparation time, I've got piles of work to do already. I haven't got time for this. I sit in the hall, and I sense I'm not the only resentful one there. We're being asked to assimilate all this information about kids we don't know yet.

This one finds large groups intimidating and won't respond well to direct questioning in front of the class. This one must always sit on your right, that's their left, and you must always face them when talking, preferably with the light falling on your face. Don't stand in front of a window. For this one you must produce a single copy of each worksheet you use 4 times as big as usual. For this one you must not write joined up and all work set must be differentiated appropriately. This one must not be confronted about lack of work, but you must also make sure he doesn't abuse his disability and get away with not pushing himself – the parents want to know immediately if you suspect this is the case. This one is on Ritalin to moderate his behaviour but we're hoping to wean him off it soon. (God, no, especially not if I have him last thing on a Friday in a Science lab).

At the end of the lesson you must make sure each of them has written their homework in their planner. Check this, or do it for them. The parents will check too. Allow plenty of time for this at the end of your lesson. But remember this one, she must leave five minutes early, with a friend, to avoid the congestion in the corridor. Each of them will have an IEP, Individual Education Plan, and to keep it simple you must set three attainable targets per pupil per lesson. (Surely this is not serious, have I misheard?) Later, staff room discussion decides that 1) sit down 2) shut up and 3) do as I say will probably not be acceptable targets. This one has a bladder problem and must be allowed to leave whenever she wishes. But you must not draw attention to this. I groan inwardly as I anticipate all the "It's not fair's" from the others looking for a brief respite from the classroom in the loos.

I'm sitting at the back, listening to all this, to these earnest professionals who totally want the best for these kids, and absolutely right too. So they should. A couple of their names I recognise from the lists I have at home of professional agencies there for David. But I'm feeling very uncomfortable. All this information is washing over me and I'm feeling a rising panic. Will I get any of these in my classes? Will I have to do all this, the extra paperwork, the enlargements, the standing in the right place, the IEPs, the targets, remembering which pair of kid gloves to don this lesson?

I can sense the atmosphere around me, the shuffling, the shifting, the body language, the barely suppressed exasperated sighs from my friends and colleagues. They want to be somewhere else, to be doing something else, something they can do and know about. Stuff they've trained for. Teaching kids (ok – *normal* kids) and getting them through exams. We're not trained for all this. Why is this all being heaped on us now? Haven't we got enough on our plates already? Is there going to be extra money? Will I be paid for this extra work? Yeah, sure, there will be support staff, classroom assistants, but not *every* lesson – you know we have to be realistic about the budget constraints – but they are always available to advise and consult and help with lesson planning. But I know this inevitably means chasing people and snatching time together at break, lunchtime and after school. There's no extra mutually agreeable time built into the timetable.

It is just assumed that we can do all this. Where are the special schools, or at least the special school teachers who know what they are doing, who are totally focussed on these children and their needs? As, indeed, they absolutely should be. But it's the other 29 kids in the class I'm worried about too. I've got to teach them as well, you know. And I'm watching myself watching my colleagues in the meeting. And I'm thinking this could be my David they're talking about in a few years' time. To my friends and colleagues I think "Don't you *dare* feel like I'm feeling now if David is in your class". And I hope things will be different with David. These teachers will know it's Sue's kid and *love* the thought of having him in their class. That they will welcome his enthusiasm and joy and want to do their utmost for him, to embrace the opportunity to give him a worthwhile challenging, fully integrated well-rounded experience of mainstream school. This is how I *hope* it will be for David. But I *suspect* that it will not.

Sue Smith

Schooling: Both Sides of the Coin

14 years ago I was a very naïve mother who knew nothing about special needs education. I remember taking my precious daughter five miles away to view a nursery in a mainstream school with special needs provision, as requested by the education department. It was large, light and well equipped but I noticed all the children in wheelchairs sat with their hands in paint, jelly or sand while the other children explored the play areas. I asked to see the headmaster, my naivety really showed when I asked him what his school had to offer my daughter. He did not appreciate the question and informed me that he had parents eagerly knocking on his door asking for their children to be admitted to his wonderful school.

I came away feeling he had taken my comments as criticism. I felt the profoundly disabled children were not supposed to take up too much of the school's time. The needs of the minority were not to infringe on the needs of the majority. This suspicion of mine was confirmed by contact with other mainstream parents of the school. And this, sadly, has been my experience of other schools, with professionals and parents alike. Change stirs up fear. I believe the ethos of a school is closely related to the personality of a headmaster and it echoes down throughout the school. I declined the place and started my education into how the system works for special needs children.

I found out that the local special needs school for physically disabled had recently been closed and all the children transferred to the school I had turned down. The closed special needs school had had a hydrotherapy pool, an excellent reputation and a nurturing environment. I could accept if this had all been moved with the children, but it had been lost.

My search took me on a 15-mile trip (same county council), to a small welcoming special school. This school oozed caring confidence and my daughter attended very happily. Shortly after this I found out about an out of county school that specialised in cerebral palsy. After a short wait, an assessment was carried out. We were very impressed with this school; it had small classes and a good ratio of staff, physiotherapist and occupational therapist assigned to each class. After a fight with the local education authority my daughter was allowed a place and I thought she would be happy until she was 19 years old. However, I was wrong. We persevered with the placement but she hated it and became withdrawn.

When my daughter was five we moved house close to a village mainstream primary school with a very good reputation. The headmaster and infant teachers agreed to accept my daughter as long as she had a one to one carer. There was no physiotherapist, occupational therapist or speech therapist 'on tap', just a class full of hustle and bustle, and my daughter blossomed very happily for three years. We forged relationships with families that have survived to this day. Lovely memories!

Sadly, the junior teachers were not so welcoming and with a very heavy heart I had to remove my daughter from the school. I knew if I had to fight to keep her at a school that didn't want her, then the fight was already lost. While we assessed the situation my daughter was home educated (5 hours per week).

When my daughter was nine years old the education department offered her a place in a newly adapted mainstream school. The local special school had been closed and all the children and care staff from the special school had been integrated into the new school. Having the special needs care staff integrated was the magic ingredient that allowed it to work. The spirit of loving care found in special education had survived and been transported to the mainstream school. Someone was getting it right, 'the baby had not been thrown out with the bath water'. My daughter enjoyed very happy times at this special mainstream school.

When it was time to leave junior school it was with a heavy heart that my daughter moved into the local mainstream secondary school, which was four miles away. This had a special needs unit attached and, sadly, care staff who didn't like my daughters independent approach to her care needs. One member of the care staff said, "I don't think you can tell me anything I don't know. I have been doing this job 10 years". This had the desired effect; my daughter kept her opinions to herself. I cannot praise the teachers enough, however: they did their best, but the school was just too big and it overwhelmed my daughter.

Settling into school wasn't helped by the fact that the threat of surgery was never far from the door. The next operation brought us to breaking point and major changes were called for. All the special schools had been closed, and we were left without any choices in our county. We moved to another county where I found a special school. This was not so much a school as an extended family. They took the time to stretch my daughter and, in their safe and secure environment, she came on leaps and bounds. It was felt that a one-day a week placement at a mainstream school would be of value. They were right; my daughter loved it, although she felt she could not cope there all week.

My daughter is 15 years of age now and can make her own choices. She has decided to go to a special needs college for the physically disabled.

A Mum

Why Do We Need Special Schools?

Special school has always been the recommended choice for my son. Hal has spent eight of his eleven years at a special school, making him (and me) something of an expert. Hal has multiple and complex disabilities: cerebral palsy, epilepsy and severe learning difficulties. Before the Education Act of 1970, Hal would have been deemed 'ineducable' and following the medical model of disability would have been cared for in a health setting. The recognition that children like Hal could benefit from school was an important step forward. Hal loves school and the exciting and challenging activities on offer all specially tailored to meet his abilities and needs.

So far so good, but thirty years after the 1970 act, the buzz-word is inclusion. I know that Hal benefits from social inclusion and from inclusive school projects like a glorious opera based on *The Thieving Magpie* led by the education team from Opera North. But now there is a radical movement for the inclusion of all children in mainstream schools, based on the claim that inclusion offers educational as well as social advantages, despite the lack of evidence to support this idea. Looking at the web-site of the Centre for Studies in Inclusive Education (CSIE), I find I cannot agree with a single one of its ten reasons for inclusion. Though full of well-meaning pieties about equality and human rights, they undervalue what I believe to be the true purpose of schooling – the development of each child's intellectual and physical talents and skills – in favour of ill-defined and dubious social benefits. They are irrelevant to Hal who would be ill-served by life in a large, mainstream school.

A special school is not a kind of ghetto for the children the world would rather forget, but rather a creative, imaginative generator of good educational practice which deserves to be more widely known. At his special school, Hal has instant access to a wide range of experts in childhood disability – an example of the multi-agency approach advocated by the government's recent special education strategy *Removing Barriers to Achievement.*

A good special school brings this group of experts together in one place for at least part of every week. Over the past eight years I have been overwhelmed by the devotion, dedication and emotional investment of the teachers, nursery nurses, assistants, administrators, cooks, taxi drivers, escorts, volunteers and fund-raisers, therapists and peripatetic experts who work together in special schools. And a good special school is greater than the sum of its parts, so that there are opportunities for staff to learn and receive from each other and from the children. Their dedication is not airy-fairy kindness, but intensely practical: staff in special schools are determined that children who face barriers shall be able to achieve their potential whatever it is. This has led to the development of measures which have meaning even if a child can 'do' very little by the standards of the non-disabled world. For example, within the last five years P-levels have been developed by special school teachers and these can measure the small changes in Hal's understanding and responses and relate them to national standards, so that Hal can be challenged in his learning.

Skills as diverse as physiotherapy, music therapy, horse-riding, augmentative communication and a mass of others make for a creative and vibrant atmosphere, often with a dose of surreal humour thrown in. I once visited the school to discover a bizarre ceremony taking place – the opening of a new kitchen cupboard in the nursery classroom, complete with satin ribbon, flowery hats and VIP guest. And I remember another, sadder occasion, the funeral of a four year old child at the school. It might have been a grim experience, but the achievements of his short life were celebrated by his teacher with such love and humour that we came away from the service uplifted rather than distressed. It is important to recognise that families and staff derive strength and solace from the shared purpose, understanding and sometimes painful experiences that make up the life of a special school.

My fear is that children like Hal, those with 'low-incidence disability' as the new easy jargon has it, could become an insignificant and forgotten minority in the bright, brave new world of inclusion for all. Hal's school career has followed almost exactly the same trajectory as the present government's period in office. David Blunkett, an unwilling special school pupil himself, rushed out a green paper *Excellence for All* within months of becoming education secretary in 1997. Though the most recent strategy for special education *Removing Barriers to Achievement* recognises that the most severely disabled children will still be educated in special schools, the radical agenda of the CSIE and the *Index for Inclusion* would prefer all such schools to be closed and the children re-located to mainstream settings.

Despite a snowstorm of consultations, initiatives, policy and legislation over the past eight years, I am far from satisfied with much of the provision available for Hal from health, social and leisure services. School has been one bright spot, one place where I have been confident that Hal is receiving the best, most appropriate input. I believe there is a vital future role for special schools, and that their role should be nurtured and extended. But if, in pursuit of utopia, these schools are lost, we shall not know until it is too late whether the experiment was worth it. Insofar as Hal can communicate his feelings, his enthusiasm and general happiness about being at school show that he is not a special school 'survivor', but a 'champion' of specialist provision.

Gillian Upton Holmes

Four Feet Taller

"Don't forget to walk down to the White Rose Ring where one of the highlights will be the Riding for the Disabled Display of Driving and Riding on Tuesday". Great Yorkshire Show Programme 2003

The Great Yorkshire Show is a prestigious highlight in the region's farming and equestrian calendar. In 2003 the Show Committee invited the Riding for the Disabled Association (RDA) to participate by organising a Riding and Carriage Driving display. On Tuesday 9th July 2003, proudly wearing my coveted blue and white RDA sweatshirt, I joined the Stockeld Park arena party. Also sporting the logo were riders and sidewalkers, grooms, drivers with their able-bodied whips and last but not least the bucket collectors. This latter group of volunteers included my disabled son Tom. I scanned the crowds in the grandstand in the hope of catching sight of him. His distinctive hobbling gait drew my eye to him as he clambered up the steps, bucket held aloft. He was doing his bit to ensure that the pleasure riding and carriage driving had given him for more than 16 years could be available to those without personal access to horses and ponies.

The collecting ring was thronged as the two driving turnouts entered and became part of the milling crowd of assorted ponies and sea of bright blue and white RDA sweatshirts. Nervous tension hung in the sweet horse scented air. As the exquisite and valuable Hackney turnouts completed their display the elegantly attired bowler hatted ring steward oversaw their exit through the arena gate. Weeks of work, effort and training were reaching fulfilment for riders, drivers and their priceless ponies. My arena party dashed in to set up the cone arrangements for Rory, Stockeld Park's grey gelding, and his turnout to execute their driving and dressage display whilst at the other end of the arena cones were being set up for Ebor group's Skewbald Pepsi and her driver.

The driving turnouts calmly circled the arena at a steady trot until the ground work was completed and then the riders and side walkers entered the arena. Bringing up the rear was Muppet, the epitome of a 'Thelwell' pony. This tiny brown Shetland was dressed in RDA regalia, including two fabric panniers hanging from his back. Muppet would assist the bucket collectors and trot along the front of the grandstand collecting his share of contributions from the public. The riders lined up facing the grandstand awaiting the signal to commence their musical ride. 'Teddy Bears Picnic' burst forth from the tannoy and off they went! In the centre of the arena riders and their mounts displayed their dressage skills with confidence as the two driving turnouts gave immaculate cone driving performances. Not a cone was displaced.

Pleasure and Benefits

Anyone viewing the display who hadn't consulted their programme or listened to the commentator may well have been unaware that this disparate group of riders, drivers and their ponies were performing under the Riding for the Disabled Association banner. Those of us who are able-bodied cannot conceive how it feels to be constrained within the confines of a wheelchair. As the ring steward chatted amiably to our arena party about the benefits of riding and carriage driving for the disabled, I hoped he was able to see for himself the joy that this unique form of therapy, and the mobility it let them experience, was giving to the participants.

It took me back to when the physiotherapist from Welburn Hall, a special school near Kirkbymoorside, North Yorkshire, had expressed a wish that severely disabled children in her care could experience the joys and benefits that my own disabled son was enjoying carriage driving with our pony Toby and myself. I responded by establishing (with a great deal of assistance) carriage driving within Welburn Hall's RDA group.

We raised initial funds with a sponsored carriage drive and Ryedale Show generously bought the special harness required. A Ruskin Ragamuffin carriage, with a folding ramp at the back enabling us to load wheelchairs, was ordered specifically to Toby's measurements. Children in Need provided the final portion of funding and we were delighted to be filmed driving as part of their next appeal. The pleasure and benefits to profoundly disabled students as they drive within the safety of Welburn Hall's beautiful grounds are inestimable and I feel privileged that they have shared their enthusiasm and will to conquer their disabilities with me.

These are children and young people who won't always reach adulthood. Carriage driving is done with and for those who have such profound and multiple disabilities that they are unable to enjoy the benefits of riding. For those children with a limited lifespan it is important that the quality of their lives, and those of the people caring for them, is as good as it can be. Organising the Carriage Driving group at Welburn Hall has meant facing the degeneration in health, and sometimes the death, of the young people with whom I have become involved. Since I have worked there I have known six young people who died before adulthood. The sadness is tempered for me by the pleasure of remembering our drives together, and driving with other children who have the same or similar needs.

A Million Miles Away

Memories come flooding back as our carriage driving group meanders through the grounds. On hot days we take to the wooded areas. Rabbits scurry to safety as we bend our way through the manicured lines of yew trees fronting the house; while the sun glistens on the lake and the statue of old father time guarding his domain. Canada geese honk fiercely as they protect their babies from the usurpers who disturb the peace of their summer idyll. We are so lucky to drive in this magical haven, a delight to the senses of the disabled and able-bodied alike. In springtime wild daffodils burst into bloom and the scent of spring blossom hangs in the air. We pass hurriedly below the rooks in case we are plopped on by them from high above where they are busy nest building, chattering noisily as they do so. As we make our way down the drive we crunch over twigs dropped as they compete to build the biggest and finest nest to house their offspring.

The reality of a world that discriminates is a million miles away as our young drivers enjoy the freedom and mobility of instant impulsion as they ask Oscar to trot on. When Toby, my own driving pony, retired Ryedale Lions and Rotary generously bought Oscar, a chunky grey driving pony for Welburn Hall where he took up residence with the riding ponies in a field near the school gates. Oscar responds instantly to commands and as we trot towards the bridge, blurry-eyed squirrels scamper for refuge up the trees.

A child without speech may utter a sound for the very first time, delighting her speech therapist who recognises the significant breakthrough in this small response. For the very first time, after weeks of coercing from dedicated physiotherapists and occupational therapists, twisted fingers may uncurl and reach for the reins. A hesitant and insecure teenager suddenly becomes more confident and daring as Oscar responds to a barely audible command and helps them discover the delights of making decisions and extending the boundaries of their world. The young man whose vision and hearing are severely impaired responds with joy when he connects with Oscar and they become a team through that sixth sense that we able-bodied helpers can only marvel at. There may even be, for some, the thrill of competing in area competitions or appearing at a show as prestigious as the Great Yorkshire Show but this is the icing on the cake.

Constant Fundraising

As I continued to extol the virtues of riding and carriage driving as a physiotherapist's tool to the Steward at the Great Yorkshire Show, I hoped he understood. But there's no substitute for seeing it for yourself. When the display came to an end beautiful huge burgundy special rosettes were presented to riders and drivers and the applause was loud and heartfelt. Weeks of preparation and training came to fruition on a memorable day in the White Rose Arena. The lengthy procedure begins of removing each pony from the carriage, then removing the sweat stained harnesses, which had been immaculate less than an hour ago, and finally bandaging each pony's legs to protect them on their homeward journey. It will be several hours before the teams will be able to put their feet up. Their final task will be to unload the ponies and turn them out to graze. Before putting their heads down to feed I'm sure Pepsi and Rory will enjoy a vigorous roll, removing all the traces of the human beings who have shared their successful day. Ponies such as Pepsi and Rory are hard to find and expensive to maintain, as are the special harnesses and carriages needed to provide a Driving for the Disabled turnout.

In the months between prestigious events such as this, which yielded £619.59p, fundraising is constant. The Welburn Hall group rack their brains for new ideas and rely heavily on the goodwill generated locally by groups such as Rotary and Lions. We are enormously grateful to them for their generosity, which enables us to do the unseen work that continues day by day within the environs of Welburn Hall. This is where small achievements become momentous steps forward and magic moments abound for profoundly disabled young people who deserve to live life to the full. This unique therapy removes some of the obstacles they encounter in everyday life and provides them with something special to look forward to on a regular basis.

Libby Fletcher

Special Education in England and Wales: A partial view

When we came to edit the final version of this book we saw that we had written relatively little about education, about making choices between special or mainstream school, or about the increasingly fraught debate around inclusion.

At first, we intended to provide a neutral history of education policy as it affects children with special needs and disabilities. These bare bones would then be fleshed out by Gillian Payne's reflections drawn both from her professional experience as a Speech and Language Therapist, and her personal view as the mother of a son with Asperger syndrome.

But we soon realised that when writing history it is not possible to be neutral. The making of statute law – from the commissioning of reports, through the drafting of Green and White Papers, the passage of the Bill through Parliament, its appearance as law and its subsequent implementation, or lack of implementation – is a political process, set by politicians, influenced by powerful lobby groups, carried out, or not, in your local school. Even describing that process involves political choices as we choose what to emphasise, what to omit. Neither of us can claim to speak for all parents, indeed we are not even speaking for the other members of our writing group, but we felt it was important to give our account of how we got to where we are now because few parents of disabled children know the history of special education in this country and most of us are unaware of the battles which have been fought, particularly over the last thirty years, to decide how and where children with special needs should be educated.

No Monopoly of Truth

Parents of disabled children hold different perspectives and political beliefs. While one parent will argue forcefully in favour of inclusion in mainstream school, another will insist that specialist separate provision is the best solution for their child. Linked by the passionate desire to see their children achieve their potential as best they can, both may be right. Some pressure groups, though, would like to enlist all parents under one banner. Over the last thirty years, the idea of 'inclusion' has come to dominate the arena of disability rights and influenced many public officials who take up the cause of disabled children. If you google 'special education' or 'inclusion' you will turn up the websites of the

Centre for Studies in Inclusive Education, Parents for Inclusion and Disability Equality in Education, all organisations which argue powerfully and emotively for inclusive education. Where these sites outline the history of special education in this country, they interpret it as moving inevitably towards total inclusion. These groups have been very influential, setting the agenda for the changes to special education we see happening today. Indeed they have been so influential that some education policy makers are convinced that there will be no special schools by the year 2020.

While the pro-inclusion groups are highly organised and very vocal, they do not speak for all disabled children or parents. And while they have helped many children to overcome barriers to a place in mainstream school, others may have been ill-served by an ideology that unquestioningly sees inclusion as good and segregation as bad.

Special schools have their passionate supporters and I am one of them. They are special places with a very remarkable mixture of practical skills and innovative educational practice. Teachers in special schools know about neurology and nappies. They roll up their sleeves and get on their knees, wipe up drool, deal with fits and still find time to stimulate and educate the children in their charge. Their approach is genuinely 'child-centred'. But can we expect the same of generalist, stressed-out teachers in a mainstream school? Even the most radical exponents of inclusion usually admit that some children (those with very complex needs) will still need specialist provision. In other words some children are just *too* disabled to benefit from inclusion. It is easy to imagine a tiny minority of special schools still struggling to fund essential adaptations for very disabled pupils as public funds are enthusiastically diverted towards inclusive projects. Then there will be a real danger that the bright new inclusive vision will force the very children who are already excluded from many opportunities even further onto the fringes of society. As the parent of a child who would fall into that category, I feel concerned that this would be a massive step backwards.

Significant Acts

Following the decision to make mass education compulsory in 1870 and the establishment of Local Education Authorities (LEAs) in 1902 the 1944 Education Act was the first occasion on which LEAs were obliged to make specific provision in special or mainstream schools for disabled children. 'Disabled children' included those with a variety of impairments: educationally subnormal and maladjusted pupils, epileptics, blind and partially sighted, deaf and hearing impaired pupils, physically handicapped and delicate pupils, " who by reason of impaired physical condition or health or educational development require a change of environment" and pupils suffering from speech defects - "stammering, aphasia, or defect of voice or articulation not due to deafness".

In 1970 the Education (Handicapped Children) Act transferred education services for disabled children from health to local authorities. The act ended the practice of classifying a minority of children (about 32,000) as 'ineducable' and removed powers to provide training for 'children who suffer from a disability of mind'. The Secretary of State for Education, Mrs. Margaret Thatcher said of this act "I am determined that these children shall take their rightful place in the educational system and receive their fair share of the resources available".

Gillian Payne: *When I started College, children with 'severe mental handicap' who were 'severely subnormal' had only recently been considered to be educable, and their care was being transferred from Health to Education services. 'Mentally retarded' was another description of these children. When I qualified in 1974, the terminology used was "Educationally SubNormal", and children were divided into two categories – ESN (M) [moderate] and ESN (S) [severe]. Many of the latter category were also "Physically Handicapped" [PH].*

The 1976 Education Act placed a duty on LEAs to educate disabled children in ordinary schools, except where it was impracticable, incompatible with efficient instruction in the schools, or if it involved unreasonable public expenditure.

Gillian Payne: *At this stage, I was working in an ESN (M) school and a Children's Psychiatric Unit (CPU). One of the clinics I covered was next to an ESN (S) school and as there was no therapy available in the school, I saw some of the children in the clinic for a while. I also became the therapist in a Language Unit, and was on the Panel that met to decide which children should be admitted to the Unit. This was my first close link with Education services other than running a clinic within schools.*

The Committee of Inquiry into the Education of Handicapped Children and Young People chaired by Mary Warnock met for over three years and reported in 1979. The Warnock Report dismissed the concept of handicap and extended the definition of special education to take in all children who had any individual educational needs. With this definition in mind the report identified that 20 per cent of children were likely to need special educational provision of some kind during their school careers. At this point approximately 2 per cent of children were in special educational provision. The report asked 'What is happening to the 18 per cent in mainstream schools?' Warnock also recognised that parents had vital information about their children that must be incorporated and used in the assessment, placement and educational process. The report saw integration as being good for some children and not for others and envisaged that some disabled children would always attend special school.

Gillian Payne: *Because I was interested in working with children with SEN (Special Educational Needs), and had developed links with Education, working jointly with several teachers, I was invited to join the forerunner of NASEN (National Association for Special Educational Needs) and a group of teachers interested in working with pre-school children with SEN. I remember attending a meeting in 1980 about the Warnock report at which we discussed the future of special schools. This was viewed fairly positively, as there would always be a need for some children to attend special schools. There would also be a need for special needs teachers to provide outreach advice to mainstream schools even if special schools did close.*

The 1981 Education Act put into practice the main recommendations in Warnock. The category 'handicapped pupil' was replaced by 'special educational needs' (SEN); each such pupil was to have a statement of SEN. Parents were to be involved in determining their child's educational needs. The act emphasised integration so that mainstream schools were responsible for identifying, assessing and providing for children with SEN.

Gillian Payne: *Although I now had a new role as a mother, I continued to attend education meetings. The feeling amongst special school staff seemed to be that they would always have a job, even if not in special schools.*

The 1988 Education Reform Act entitled every pupil (including those with SEN) to a broad and balanced curriculum (the National Curriculum) even though a small number of pupils might need adaptations and special arrangements. However, schools were worried that they did not have enough guidance on identifying and assessing special educational needs and this led to inconsistent provision across the country.

Gillian Payne: *By this stage I was working part-time, and had to learn yet more new terminology. Children had a moderate or severe learning disability – they were not 'disabled.' My son was having difficulty in conforming to the school's expectations of him. It was easier to get help for his physical problems than his behavioural and learning difficulties.*

In 1992 the Audit Commission and Her Majesty's Inspectorate report on special needs provision identified weaknesses and a lack of consistency in the way in which children with special needs were identified and provided for. These failures included statements which took too long to complete and were vague, no guaranteed provision for special needs, lack of accountability and resources and disorganised annual reviews.

Gillian Payne: *Hurrah! My son finally has a statement! I agreed to postpone the process for a year, but as things were not improving, pushed for the magic piece of paper that would facilitate extra provision. I have had to do a lot of thinking and writing about all the most negative things about my son – this has made me very frustrated and despondent, but at least he will get a computer and typing lessons, and additional support in class. Perhaps his teacher won't look so stressed all the time, and I won't have to visit her in the classroom every week to learn about his latest misdemeanours! This will be a big help for us.*

The 1993 Education Act Introduced the Code of Practice on the identification and assessment of SEN. The code required LEAs to help schools identify any child with SEN and give additional support where needed. Eight regional SEN tribunals were set up under the Education Act 1993 for parents to appeal against LEA decisions on special educational provision – the first case was heard in 1995.

Gillian Payne: *At the annual review before leaving primary school, I was told that because my son had made good progress with the extra support, it was to be withdrawn. Why? Surely it proves how beneficial the help has been. However, he would have a learning support tutor in his class at secondary school, and would "have access" to help from her. This tutor would be on hand to support him in science and design and technology lessons, in which he might pose a danger to himself or others.*

After a term in secondary school, my son was becoming disaffected. [He was always late for lessons, got lost, and was not doing all of his homework]. The Special Educational Needs Advisory Panel (SENAP) recommended that he should "continue to have access to school-based resources" (i.e. he would not have any individual support). I was quite pleased when I read in this letter that this support would be provided until the Special Needs Co-ordinator (SENCo) phoned to express her concern, and clarified what the SENAP meant! I therefore wrote to reinforce my concerns, and received a reply that really annoyed me. My son would get individual support because I had requested it so articulately. This was NOT fair on other families. I was also embarrassed that I had not understood the implications of the wording of the original letter.

As it happens, even this extra help was not sufficient for my son and he later attended a special school, at which he thrived.

I was sad to find that, despite my son having been provided with a laptop computer, this was kept locked in the Special Needs room, as it was considered that it would be too dangerous for him to carry around the school with him. He was still waiting for the typing lessons outlined in his statement. The 'magic' piece of paper was developing some weaknesses!

My son was now attending a school for boys with 'specific learning difficulties'. This term embraced the spectrum of dyslexic-type disorders. This very special school was structured, with strict routines and expectations, and suited my son. I was delighted with this placement, and my son was happy and enjoyed going to school – even at 7:15 on Monday morning as a weekly boarder. Because he was away at school, he had less contact with local peers.

The 1996 Education Act was full of the buzzwords of the 1990s – choice, transparency and accountability. It introduced clear guidelines for identification and assessment of SEN (the 5 stage Statementing process). The main aspects of the act were as follows:

1. A Code of Practice giving detailed guidance to schools and LEAs on identifying, assessing, recording, meeting, and reviewing SEN. A 26-week time limit to complete the process of issuing a legally binding statement of SEN. LEAs had to review statements according to procedures laid down in the Act. LEAs had a duty to assess and provide for children with statements of SEN from the age of two or earlier if they had been identified as having SEN.

2. Rights: Parents of children with statements were able to choose a maintained school for their child and (subject to certain conditions) the LEA had to agree. Parents' rights to appeal against LEA decisions to an independent SEN Tribunal were extended

3. Schools: The maintained school named on a child's statement of SEN had to accept that child. Schools had a duty to draw up, publish, and report on their SEN policy.

Gillian Payne: *I don't think I have ever seen an IEP (Individual Education Plan) for my son, and the annual review process was not carried out according to the Code of Practice. I have now trained as a "Named Person"; an independent volunteer trained to support parents through the statementing process. Should I rock the boat by complaining that the laid-down process is not being followed in our case? On balance, I decide to stay silent – after all, my son is happy, and learning well. His writing is now legible – this is due to an hour's writing practice every morning. I start to think about the transitional review, which should decide his future education. I can't imagine him leaving school next year to attend a mainstream college. The Careers Advisor is consulted, and recommends specialist college or an independence unit.*

The green paper *Excellence for all children: meeting special educational needs* was one of David Blunkett's first actions when he became Minister for Education following the Labour Party's victory in the 1997 general election. The paper focused attention on parent partnership, planning, training for teachers and learning support assistants (LSAs), and the new buzzwords of 1997, 'inclusion', 'rights' and 'joined-up thinking'.

Gillian Payne: *I contributed to consultations on this, as a parent and as a member of NASEN. It feels good to be asked to contribute ideas – and I have been forthright about my support for special schooling for children with behaviour problems. I am currently pushing for a diagnosis of Asperger syndrome for my son, as I hope this will entitle him to support in his increasingly awkward adolescent years. I think he is now officially considered to have 'additional needs', whatever they might be.*

In 1999 the government published a White Paper on how special education was going to develop, *Meeting special educational needs: a programme of action*. It identified inclusion as the 'keystone' of education policy and pointed out the 'educational, social and moral' benefits of inclusion. Did all these words carry equal weight and importance?

Gillian Payne: *My son has a place at the Independence Unit at another special school. It takes some time to sort out his new statement, as the transitional review process went awry. However eventually we get a little documentation, and after almost a year he is officially in the Unit.*

What is meant by 'inclusion'? The word doesn't exist in my dictionary. How do you 'include' children who have challenging and disruptive behaviour and learning disabilities (or do I mean difficulties – it seems the terms are interchangeable these days) in the context of lack of teacher training? Half a day's INSET is not going to equip people to be experts on disorders like autism! So many teachers are stressed by the constantly changing guidelines, curriculum, extra record keeping and SATS. How do they cope with all the pressures from Government and Education? It's difficult enough coping with the changes in the NHS in my job without having to bone up on special needs legislation and regulations! As a

Speech and Language Therapist I have to "have regard" to the Code of Practice in making recommendations and setting targets for children. Work and home life seem to be merging more closely, even without my voluntary agency interests!

Another new term that seems to have emerged is 'differently abled' – is this from the social model of disability, or a politically correct usage?

A new emphasis on human rights began to emerge in the late 1990s. The Disability Rights Task Force 1999 report *From Exclusion to Inclusion* recommended that the Disability Discrimination Act 1995 be extended to education, later in 1999 the Disability Rights Commission was established to help secure civil rights for disabled people. The year 2000 saw the publication of the *Index for Inclusion* by the Centre for Studies in inclusive Education (CSIE). The *Index* was a document to support the inclusive development of mainstream schools and was placed by the Government in every school and LEA in England. Key concepts of the document included the idea that educators should remove 'barriers to learning and participation', provide 'support for diversity' and claims that inclusion is an ideal and 'a way of improving schools according to inclusive values'. Educators are encouraged to develop 'reflective practice' and become more inclusive. The vocabulary is that of moral discourse.

The *Index* was developed at the same time as another big idea in educational policy at the time – the standards agenda which was concerned with standards and excellence. But is there in fact a conflict between these two ideas? Can you really have an inclusive culture and academic excellence in the same school?

Gillian Payne: *'Named persons' are now 'Independent Parental Supporters', another new title.*

This year has been a nightmare. Because annual reviews were not carried out correctly and there was a lack of documentation, my son has been turned down by Social Services for funding at a college for young people with Asperger syndrome. Despite my writing several 'articulate' reports, using the complaints procedure, finding an advocate to help my son express his feelings and gaining strong support from his Independence Unit, my son has not been able to access the college he hoped to attend. The local mainstream college felt that they could not offer an appropriate level of support for his ability level, and recommended specialist provision. In the end we have reluctantly settled for a place at a college for people with moderate to severe learning disabilities. As my son does not officially qualify for support from the Learning Disability Service on the grounds that his IQ is too high, this seems rather incongruous. As his diagnosis was made through this team, he is still under their umbrella.

I find it hard to write work reports now. I must get the terminology right, and set "SMART" targets for children on my caseload. I now know from bitter experience what can happen if things are not properly documented, or insufficient evidence is collected at the right stages.

In 2001 the Special Educational Needs and Disability Act (SENDA) Part 1 amended the 1996 Education Act. This act was launched under the banner of 'Excellence for All' – the vocabulary of standards was appropriated for inclusion. It begs the question will this really lead to excellence for all children, or mediocrity? The act imposed new duties on LEAs and schools.

1. Code: A new Code of Practice, identification and assessment of SEN was changed from the five part process to School Action and School Action Plus and extended to early years as well.
2. Rights: LEAs had to provide and advertise parent partnership services and arrange to resolve disputes between parents and schools/LEAs without affecting parents' right of appeal to the Tribunal, the title 'Named Person' was changed to Independent Parental Supporter (IPS). Schools were required to inform parents when any SEN provision was made for their child. SENDA set out clearer guidance for appeals to the Tribunal, including time limits.
3. Inclusion: new Statutory Guidance on the practical operation of the framework for inclusion, *Inclusive Schooling: Children with Special Educational Needs* and a SEN Toolkit for schools/LEAs.

In 2002 SENDA Part 2 amended the 1995 Disability Discrimination Act and covered access to education. The intention was to strengthen the rights of disabled children to a place in the school of their choice and was formulated against the background of a general strengthening of disabled rights and the creation of the Disability Rights Commission. It was now unlawful for schools and post-16 education settings to discriminate against a disabled person in admission arrangements, provision of education and associated services, or exclusions. LEAs had to plan to increase accessibility for disabled pupils in terms of the curriculum, the physical environment and information. The SEN Tribunal was renamed the SEN and Disability Tribunal (SENDIST) and its remit was extended to cover cases of disability discrimination.

Gillian Payne: *There are rumours that statements may be withdrawn. There will be school-based provision of support for children with SEN.*

Unfortunately small schools are likely to do badly under the new system – our county has a lot of tiny rural schools. County is concerned that there may be an increase in the number of appeals and tribunals, as parents fear the loss of the entitlements given by statements. There has been a review of special needs provision, and it is rumoured that some special schools will close because of the push for inclusion. Who will miss out? Which schools are to go? More consultations are held. One day I attend two meetings, one as a member of staff working in schools and another as a parent. The mood at the parents' meeting is tense and anxious. How will things work out? There is a lot of fear and concern around.

In fact I never had much feedback about that Special Education Review, but another round of consultation has recently started, so I guess it's a matter of 'Watch this space!' I think the views of parents are taken more seriously now, and that parent support groups have helped this to move forward. Changes are still frequent and far-reaching, and too fast for comfort.

2005 Some statements have been withdrawn, but support of children has been continued by schools. Parents are worried that children may lose their entitlement to provision. It is too early to know yet. There is confusion from parents and school staff, but there is a sense of goodwill. However, because teaching assistants are now based in classrooms and not so closely attached to particular children, I feel some concern as to who will be able to back up speech therapy work in the classroom, as the assistants seem to be working all the time with groups of children.

As I write this, in October 2005, the ideological tide seems to be on the turn. Baroness Warnock now regrets the educational consequences of her enthusiasm for inclusion and integration back in the 1970s, calling it a "disastrous legacy." In her pamphlet *Special Educational Needs: a New Look* published in 2005, by the Philosophy of Education Society of Great Britain, she calls for a radical review of the closure of special schools, arguing that pressure to include children with special needs had led to "confusion, of which children were the casualties." Disability organisations remain tight-lipped, but a 2005 survey in Scope's magazine *Disability Now* revealed that 97 per cent of its readers rejected the idea of total inclusion.

In the meantime, local authorities are pressing ahead with the closure of special schools, some parents are choosing home education, demanding specialist units or setting up private schools for children whose needs are not being met. Children will have been consulted at the end of 2005 about their experience of inclusion. The special education merry-go-round continues to spin. And parents and children alike in the families with disabled children will be spun round with it. Some will enjoy the ride, some will never manage to jump on board; others will fall off and hurt themselves while others will stagger, sick and dizzy, back onto firm ground. It feels very uncomfortable to be questioning inclusion: surely it is a good thing, a desirable thing? But the obsessive and unilateral focus on inclusion sometimes feels very dishonest, too concerned with the big idea to worry about the small, essential, practical details. Unless inclusion works, and there is no evidence that it does work all the time, for all or even most disabled children, it will be even more damaging than the system it replaces.

However, the purpose of this article is not to persuade you to our way of thinking. Rather, by outlining the changing approaches to special education we hope to show you that there is no one right or inevitable form of provision. The statutory decisions that shape educational provision for disabled children are subject to debate, influence and change. We hope to encourage you to explore the issues as fully as you can, so that you are able to evaluate decisions concerning your child's education from an active and informed standpoint.

Gillian Upton Holmes

Gillian Payne

Inclusion and Confusion

I have developed some strong views on inclusion, difference, diversity and tolerance. In the educational context, I think inclusion should mean an appropriate education for all, based on individual planning, and paying regard to the views of the child and carers as far as possible. I have trained with the Local Education Authority as an independent parental supporter, which enables me to support and guide parents through the statementing and annual review processes. A statement of special educational needs defines and determines the support that should be given to a child in school. I do try to make sure that young people have their say in this process too. Parents and children may not agree and this must be respected, although as an opinionated parent myself at times I appreciate how hard this can be.

Which Hat Am I Wearing?

I have been able to form links and to build up communication between health, education and voluntary organisations. I am a professional and parent member of the Autism Task Group, and have collected views from parents about service development, and presented these to the group. Ryedale Special Families' autism and ADHD support groups have been involved with consultations with the Primary Care Trust and I also belong to an Asperger Network trying to set up services for young people and adults with Asperger syndrome. I have given talks to speech and language therapy colleagues about my experiences both as a parent of children with communication disorders and as a child with motor problems. I have also taken part in forums at a local and national level, particularly with reference to ADHD and autism. I sometimes feel there is a conflict between my various roles, especially the personal and professional, and find it helpful to identify which "hat" I am wearing so that I can express my opinion appropriately and effectively.

Parents still describe the process of working to ensure that their child receives good support as a battle, which leaves them feeling negative. I often stand on my metaphorical soapbox and state that parents and professionals have a tremendous amount to offer each other. Parents seek out information about their child's specific disorder and how to access support services, which teachers, doctors, therapists and social care staff are often best placed to provide, but it is the parents who know how their offspring tick. They live with their children's disorders every day of their lives and this gives them a different but equally important knowledge, which, if it were properly valued by the professionals, would surely make the world of disability more inclusive. Parents normally appreciate the opportunity to learn more about the nature of and support for their children's disorders but need childcare to enable them to join in properly. When parents are able to gain a greater understanding of how "the system" works they are often more tolerant of the glitches that can occur, but are also empowered to negotiate for a better system. Parents are a valuable resource in consultations, but these consultations ought to be arranged at mutually convenient times, not just to suit the professionals. There is also scope for parents to help in preparing general and child-specific training packs for teachers, health and care services as they have often developed their own strategies to enable their child to function as well as possible.

The Special Educational Needs Code of Practice states that all teachers are teachers of special needs children, and should be able to include all children in their teaching. However, little training on special needs is offered to student teachers, and there is such a diversity of problems, that it is hard to see how teachers can possibly feel prepared for every possible difficulty. This is where I feel that advice and outreach work from special school staff or health service staff can be helpful. When I worked in a language unit, the teacher and I both planned together, then worked with the whole class or small groups, or with individuals. She knew which speech sounds or sentence structures were targets, and I would relate my work to the current topic. To demonstrate new vocabulary, we often worked together. We accepted other children from the school who needed extra help with language into the class and sent some of the unit children into mainstream classes for integration. This was well before inclusion was a government initiative.

A Brilliant Concept But ...

Inclusion is a brilliant concept, but it is most successful with those who are easy to include. Children with social and behavioural difficulties, and those with poor self-esteem, who have endured negative feedback and constant failure, are hard to include. My son used to be disruptive – if he had not remembered or understood what he was supposed to be doing, he wandered round the classroom scribbling on other children's work. He was tiny and looked sweet and innocent, and got away with a lot, but must have been a nightmare for his teachers. As he became older, he became more aware of his problems with co-ordination, learning and understanding, and became more disaffected with life at school. He only survived because his sister and her friends intervened when he was distressed. He found the transfer to secondary school very challenging. He had problems with organising his belongings, knowing which lesson and which classroom he should be in, did not know if the bells signified the beginning or end of lessons and, above all, had to cope with a different member of staff for each subject. He used to be awarded a smiley face sticker if he was less than ten minutes late for the start of a lesson, but he was unable to catch up and spent the rest of the lesson with no idea of what was going on. This was not inclusion, however hard the special needs staff tried to help him.

It is paradoxical that I, who believed in the value of inclusion, decided that my son's needs would be best met in special school. He flourished at Netherside Hall, where there were about forty-five boys with specific learning difficulties who had found mainstream school hard to cope with. The staff worked closely together and life was very structured. The boys were given plenty of opportunity to develop skills – my son would not have been included at his mainstream school in canoeing, climbing, potholing or skiing activities – and his self-esteem rose considerably as he discovered that, with help, he could manage all of these. The boys were also encouraged to work towards their bronze life-saving awards in swimming. This fostered my son's interest in sport.

At sixteen, he left Netherside Hall to attend an Independence Unit, which was part of Welburn Hall School. Again he blossomed in the special environment. Sometimes I feel now that he is *too* confident, and a little unrealistic about his abilities. However I do think a sheltered environment, in which he was valued for himself, has led to greater inclusion in the community than he would have had in the mainstream environment, in which he was always so conscious of all his failings.

As I think about inclusion in education, I would like to see that everyone's background and experiences are taken into account. Children with disabilities can be branded like a Czech friend of my parents, who overcame the horrors of her time in Auschwitz concentration camp, and the permanent tattoo which marked her time there, to move to a new country where she was totally accepted by her peers. She was able, because of her personality and the support she received, to move on to live a happy and fulfilled life and to bring others to an understanding and acceptance of difference. I look forward to inclusion being the norm but accept that for some children special education will always be more appropriate.

Gillian Payne

7 Making Sense Of It All

Star Boy

One of the features of Down's Syndrome is the stubby hand, with shorter than normal fingers.

He is no longer here but here he sits with me, forever. Radiant in his smile, in his comforting presence, in his raised hand. I can see him, by just looking on the mantelpiece at his photograph as it imperceptibly crumples and fades in the sunshine.

Here he sits with me in the garden, forever radiant in his smile but I cannot see him. Very rarely, through the mists, I can sense his presence or I can turn back time and recall a precious, forgotten moment. But just once, in the four years since he left us, did I feel him so tangibly close, so central to our family, forever one with us. It was when his younger brother was being baptised. Shuffling and smiling, he seemed to be standing with us, as the half circle of the altar rail enveloped our small family. Just a month before he died, he had been there for his own christening, charming the congregation with his smiles. Some bonds cannot be broken by death. The oneness of love and family seemed unbreakable before the humility and eternity of the altar. He will always be a son, always a brother, always the first-born and always part of our family. And I will be his father for eternity.

Today I can no longer see his racked body, the heart scar, his proud medal of his short war with life. But I can see his perfections. His tubby baby-tummy and his fine, flyaway curls. His ears, not exorbitant like adult ears, not the flaps of *real* babies, but small, the perfect size. All babies should have ears like this. They are the definitive baby ears, denied to real babies. The clear perfect skin, not what I had expected at his birth – no blotches, no eczema, not fragile, not reptilian, but smooth as silk. *Real* babies should have such skin. But best of all, the perfect hand, held up now in blessing in this fading, old photograph. The diminutive hand whose fingers appear like the points of a star, perfectly proportioned, symmetrical – perfect hand that was snatched away from me at birth to be incubated. But this was my first connection with him – tickling each of his tiny fingers through the gauze, hoping to stimulate his dexterity at one-hour-old.

His far-away, rayed hands which became so dextrous, waving his two rattles in unison, so intently surveying a toy and so gently stroking my hair as I snoozed. And now his graceful photograph-hand eternally raised in a loving wave, a smiling welcome, a forever blessing. *Real* babies have their long, straddling claw-fingers, gripping, grasping, grabbing, as they will in their long lives. All babies should have star fingers.

He sits with me here on a train – the photograph now a hundred miles away, as I yearn for the tiny, warm hand that was snatched away too soon. My star boy. How I would hold your hand again.

John Smith

The raven

I decided to wrap it up in tissue paper,
tie it up with string,
put it in an old battered suitcase,
pull down the steps from the loft,
climb up them and push open the hatch,
clamber across the rafters and hide it
behind all the other old and battered suitcases.
It would stay there, sorted.

For months I carried on
smiling sunnily at the world,
convinced that all was well.
I enjoyed the clouds,
grinned at the rain,
sang to the trees,
rose in the morning tired, but not lethargic,
I barely glanced upwards to the loft.

But one morning I heard a rustling,
just audible, from up above.
I didn't look, didn't investigate.
"Just a sparrow under the tiles"
I said to myself.

My limbs felt heavy, my head felt dull,
my neck was stiff and painful
but still I sang to the trees.
The damson trees suggested I was a little off key.
Who, me?
At night I tossed and turned
In the morning, I rose troubled and aching.

It got harder not to look
but the imp of the perverse was winning.
The tapping grew louder.
Now, a steady drumming elicits a response.

If I put my earplugs in, how long can I pretend
there is nothing in my loft?
I succumb to the inevitable. My time is up.
I've had eight months of respite, of singing to the trees.
I pull down the steps to the loft, climb up them,

push open the hatch.
He's sitting there, shreds of tissue paper
in his feathers and his beak. He blinks knowingly.
Stretches his wings.
Takes flight. Lands. He's back.
My big black raven of despair.

Libby Fletcher

Dealing with God

When I was first told I was carrying a baby with Down's Syndrome, I felt horrified at the huge lump, the deformity, the stigma, the dirty shame I would be humping about on my belly. Now I walk around feeling like a half person who will never fit in again or fully engage in life again, never connect again. There is a tape in my head – "I had a baby. That baby had Down's, that baby died".

A Shameful Lump

I resigned myself to carrying this deformed and shameful lump around in front of me, but secretly tried to do a deal with God – okay God, it's in your hands. I've been the virtuous Christian standing up for what is right and being incredibly brave and noble, and everyone's seen I'm not deliberately going to kill this baby but perhaps if I were to miscarry then everything would be okay. Nature, you would have sorted it out and it would all be "for the best". If I felt a twinge, I'd long for it to get worse. If I went to the loo, I longed to see blood. I wanted it to be sorted, to be taken away, but I did not want the responsibility – the blood on my hands. But you weren't going to make it that easy for me were you God? Oh no. Your "plan", your "will" (if I believe you have these), was far less simple, far more complicated. Massive, messy, repercussive, all encompassing.

That Little Baby

That little baby was born. That little baby was a little person. That little baby was so beautiful, so brave. That little baby survived his heart surgery and came home with us and made us a family. That little baby smiled and loved and changed everything. And then that little baby died. Where is the point in that? Why couldn't he have gone before he was born? That was my plan God. It made sense to me. Why put us through this? From Hell to Heaven and back to Hell? When we had him, I knew I'd done a U-turn, or a U-turn had happened to me. David was my boy, my son, my baby.

This was our little world. I'd found a place in it, a place in Down's world, a lovely place. A hard place of toil and struggle and pain, yes; but also a place of fun and joy and hope. A place of seismic attitude shifts and life changes. We were on our way! On a journey! This wasn't what I had expected God, but it would do! Yes it would! I was to be David's Mum, and we were going to change our little corner of the world. We were going to be ambassadors for Down's Syndrome, carry the torch, fly the flag, dance and march along in our own little parade. Yeah! Yippee!

Thank you God, yes, really, thank you, you do move in mysterious ways but yeah, I can handle this. I didn't realise it was going to be like this, so lovely, so David. The hospital stays, the chest x-rays, the heart scans, the medication, the scares? Well, they were all part of it, the journey to the future, laying the foundations. Things to be got through on our way, obstacles to be overcome. And that last time, in intensive care, David, you were going to pull through. We prayed. God can, and will, work a miracle. We'll get back on our feet again and carry on. And even when the nurse was calling more and more urgently for some fluid that you needed, when the curtains came round, and people appeared and they pumped and pumped you full of drugs and the Doctor kept on trying to resuscitate you, saying "Come on David, come on David" with tears in his eyes and the machines were clanging and the numbers on the screen were dropping and dropping, I still thought there was time for the miracle to happen. This horror, just like the stuff they call drama you can see most nights on TV, couldn't really be happening, not to us, not to our David. The nurse said "I think its time now" and suddenly all the tubes were whipped out and the sensors off, and you, little David, were in our arms, warm and floppy and asleep. You died very soon then, I think, slipped away, cuddled by Mummy and Daddy – ironically, the cuddle we couldn't give you at your birth when you were whipped away to Special Care.

Fallout

And afterwards people said: Maybe it was for the best. Didn't you expect it might happen? You couldn't have gone on could you? You made a mistake in loving him too much. What? What? No, no no! How dare they even try to make sense of this! There is no way to make sense of this, to tell me what is for the best, to make it okay, paint over the cracks or to dumb down the horror or to put it all away neatly in a pretty box. It should not have happened and that is it. Live with it. Live with the confusion and horror and shattered world. Sorry if it upsets your comfy world where everything happens for a reason and is explained and 'for the best'.

You see, God, it would have been so much simpler if I had miscarried. Same result in the end: Dead baby. But not all this fallout. This toxic emotional shrapnel. What was the point? Was it to make me a better person? Ha! Don't feel better. To show me what is important in life? Hasn't worked. Still don't know. Make me a stronger person? Hasn't worked. Feel even weaker. Makes no sense. Full stop.

Sue Smith

My Ball of Pain

I woke one morning to find it hammering at my door, trying to get in. Foolishly, I opened the door a crack, allowing it to enter. Within minutes it had attached itself to my ankle. Since then, I've hauled it up hill, down dale wondering all the while why it was invisible to all those who passed by. Usually they glance furtively at the sweat pouring down my brow then scurry away in rat-race haste, in pursuit of happiness. So, disenchanted with the human race, I tugged at my chain and the ball of pain trailed along behind bumping into me whenever I headed downhill. I've tucked it under the duvet with me when I've heaved myself exhausted into bed. I've pleaded with it not to appear in my dreams. Waking in the night I've leapt out of bed, only to find it still attached to my ankle.

I'm going over the final summit now. If I find the key and release it, where will it go? Will it roll onward, gathering momentum, and attach itself to an unsuspecting person innocently passing by? Or will I find myself running after it, unable to bear the weightlessness of its absence?

If only I could leave it for half-an-hour outside the pub with a notice: – No walkers, no bikers, no dogs, no children, no balls of pain. Would a masochist steal my huge and irresistible cannon ball of pain? Would I be left desolate and inconsolable? If I leave it outside a supermarket will it spot a blithe, free spirit cooing over her tiny baby in its pram, introducing it to the outside world? And will it attach itself triumphantly to another soul?

Then I'd have a millstone of guilt to carry on my shoulders, along with all the other guilt that weighs me down. If I do wake one morning to find myself unencumbered what will I do? Pinch myself in disbelief? Sigh with relief when I hear it hammering at my door pleading desperately to be let in?

What would I do?

What would you do?

Libby Fletcher

George

January 2000

You look at me so trustingly
You grab me as I pass
Your presence speaks volumes
Will this feeling last?
My patience grows from loving you
My kindness is wider
My empathy real
I love you so much George
Do you really love me?
Will you tell me one day?
Will I ever really know?
I believe you do
I am special to you
I am grateful for your being
Words cannot express the things I feel inside
How can I describe these feelings inside?
I do not know … and I do not mind not knowing

Lesley

A Mum

Who is this woman that signs herself mum? She is not an intellectual or an academic. She wiles away her time listening to and nurturing her intuition. Trying to be practical but finds herself baffled by modern technology and increasingly drawn to the simple wild things of life. Welcoming mind stretching experiences, yet shrieking with pain when deeply hurt and then angry as life wallops her, knocking her clean off her polished pedestal, which has happened on many occasions. She tries to leave out the ingredient blame and grows, using such events as a tool for new understanding, learning that the most painful experiences in life can be the biggest learning curve. And she is learning to say 'Thank you', coming to the realisation that the depths of unimaginable opportunity are endless. She is a woman who will turn away from conflict, waiting with an open heart to grasp the value of healing in another direction.

A Mum

Little Wellington Boots

I imagine them in a neat row. Or maybe a messy pile. Tossed there by boys who have to go now urgently and be pirates or knights in the attic playroom. Mud covered after an afternoon romping through the woods. Squelching along the shore of the lake. Lying face down staring through a hole in the broken jetty to watch tadpoles and stickleback dart in the water below. Tramping up into the bluebell wood to see rabbits and bring home armfuls of fir cones.

Those were the sort of scenes I imagined when I was pregnant with my second child.

Later would come school and rugby and beach holidays in Pembrokeshire or Devon. Multi-generational games of cricket, university friends and their children. Hard work, prizes, satisfaction and contentment, the pleasures and rewards of a job well-done.

Well perhaps it was a little fanciful. That Famous Five, scrubbed and polished, 1950s vision of perfect Family Life. Fanciful for me at least, as I was then, intense, dissatisfied in a marriage and social environment that I was beginning to find oppressive, seeing, out of the corner of my eye, somewhere over there, another more authentic life I could live. But in another way, a harmless enough fantasy, and a common one, and one shared by many people.

That bright imagined future was shattered when Hal was diagnosed with severe cerebral palsy. The dream was revealed as no more than feeble denial of the painful realities of life, and the belief that I could have what other people seemed to enjoy so easily, as a laughable fantasy.

Few people said anything particularly horrible to me. But silence and avoidance, a phone that doesn't ring and invitations that fail to arrive, and friends who find it all too much to cope with, are more eloquent than any number of stupid, cruel remarks.

Those little wellington boots are a symbol of independence. In them the toddler begins to master the world. In them, he can splash in puddles, squish mud, conquer continents of snow. He can watch in wonder as the sea rolls up over the boots and then back again on a bright December afternoon in Scarborough

I had carefully saved the little wellington boots as T. grew out of them. His first red ones, then a blue pair, then green with toes like a frog's face. Finally I realised that Hal would have no use at all for them.

Gillian Upton Holmes

8 Loss, Bereavement and Moving On

To put it in a nutshell

If you are frightened, don't disempower yourself by using the old security networks conditioned into you as a child; they never worked anyway. Just look at your parents. 'God bless and love them all, they did their best'. Don't blame others. Don't blame yourself. That simply pours in more pain. Try a new gentle way, be a pioneer; try it.

We all pour pain into the same place, shut in by fear, we all know the look of fear on another's face: that look we shy away from. To face it is to touch our pain, do it when you're ready, one day. Until then, pat yourself on the back for surviving so well this far. Own it, acknowledge your feelings to yourself first. The most important step of all has just been taken. Take responsibility: don't wait to be offered it. Own what you need to own, feel what you need to feel, love, cherish and value your feelings enough to speak your truth to yourself first. Strange isn't it, we all know how to own happiness, we shout it from the rooftops. Why are we so ashamed of our hidden emotional pain? Perhaps we could explore this another time, now it is time to close the nutshell.

A Mum

Extracts from my Diary after David's Death

7 Nov 2000

Approaching the first anniversary of David's death I am so frightened and bewildered. I'm churning and churning in my stomach and heart and head. I feel completely cut adrift, tossed and turned by everything and anything, desperately searching for *some* meaning, some certainty, some "sign", some direction, some future. I feel very, very alone. The fear paralyses me sometimes. So do the voices, the chattering monkeys, the white noise, badly tuned radio in my head. I just want to turn the volume down sometimes.

And, like John, I think I'm frightened to even try to let go of the fear to God because I'm very frightened of God and he should be my Rock, my refuge, my strength etc. etc. But what if he isn't? What then? Nothing to cling to, just a swirling black confusing abyss. It's so hard to make sense of anything. One day I think I've found some sort of answer, some sort of direction, then next day it seems meaningless.

8 Nov 2000

David, look David; look at all those things . . . .

Remembering my excitement and joy and getting David excited and inquisitive, raising his head, looking round, following with eyes, smiling, wonderment.

You would be two now, what a big boy. You wouldn't be a *baby;* you would be a *boy.* What would you be eating? Would you be crawling? – Hope so. Little fat thighs and bottom wriggling and wobbling on the floor. Would you be talking to us? Well, more than you did? You had started "mamama", "bababa", "rururuRU", and "Ah" when you were excited, interested and intent, when you wanted to see us do something again, or when there was a gap in the "conversation" and it was your turn to communicate. And your lovely raspberries. The time you copied your Daddy with your "Ah-boo" was so magical, a sure sign that you were in fact a very bright baby, that you were so keen to learn and copy and communicate. Thank you for doing that for your Daddy. It meant a lot to us both. I was so proud, almost tearful. That was soon after you came home. You would have been six months old. We are so sad that Bev, your health visitor, is leaving, she was so much part of you when you came home. She was involved in so much of your life. I can imagine her saying "Hello David". Still, how proud I feel at the mention of you, and your name.

Last week Daddy and I went to our friends from church for a meal. They thanked God for your happy face, for you bringing joy to the hosts in Heaven! Are you David? Are you really? Are you happy and safe? Can I be sure? Can we *safely* let you go, knowing you are safe. My little Darling, my little boy, my little son, my little pal. Little squidgy baby with beaming round face, little bottom, chunky thighs, smooth palms and soles of feet, little tiny nails I cut, little new curls and little new baby teeth. How proud I was to find your first teeth.

And how proud I was when we went to Kirkbymoorside Playgroup Open Day. You were so bright and alert and interested in all the *things!* (I bet I was whispering to you to look at all the things). I was excited with you, for you. The play leader took you round too, to have a look, she held you. You got a bit grumpy and this is such a precious memory, the first time I can remember you wriggling round and putting your arms out towards me, reaching for *me*, your *Mummy*. I felt so intimate with you then David, so much that I was special to you, such a *bond*. I was your Mummy, – role and purpose. A treasured memory which I *enjoy* thinking about. I remember your wriggles. I remember you on your changing mat, wriggling to clatter the handle on the drawer. I have a physical, bodily memory of it when I'm at the gym, on one of the multipresses. I lie on my back and stretch and wriggle to alter the weights. I feel like you! I think of you and sometimes I feel my face is like yours. I am so proud that I can see my face in yours, yours in mine. It's when I'm sort of looking downwards, or along my body when I'm horizontal, sticking my chin out. There is a picture of you in your cot with that chinny look.

Oh David, we would have done so many things, as well as seeing so many things. Playgroup. I was so proud of you when you "got in" – like you'd got straight A's and were going to medical school. Also, so proud getting the letter saying that you had been 'accepted' on to the Portage scheme and the speech therapy; hearing reports describing you as a bright, alert, playful little boy – such pride. These were things said before you died, so somehow more meaningful.

Oh yes, things we would have done – playgroup, swimming, Mums'n'tots, holidays, crawling, walking. I wanted to walk with my little toddler son David on one of my favourite local walks, holding his hand and showing him all the things! It keeps coming up but I just loved it David, showing you and talking to you about all THE THINGS! I had this vision while I was pregnant with you David, while I was on that walk. I knew you had Down's, but I had already begun to picture you, and sing in my head "Best Baby in the Universe, little David John". I had named you too. And that was your name when you were born. Such a lovely name.

David, David, David, so hard to make sense of it. I don't know – I don't know anything. Where are you? Are you there? Are you happy and safe? Have you seen Jesus? What about your little brother or sister who started in the wrong place in the ectopic pregnancy? Look after each other. Do you know why that happened? That's silly, asking a baby. I don't think I want David to know or understand these things. I have to ask God, and his son Jesus, and for the Holy Spirit to make it clear. Or give me the grace to be calm about it. Give me the grace I need to pray. But sometimes I have so *little* hope, to dare to ask. I cannot understand what has happened in the past, so am scared of what will happen. More of the same? To lose another baby? To have another disastrous pregnancy? To lose John? Or something I can't even imagine yet? (I never imagined the last two plus years – they still happened).

9 Nov 2000

Little tiny David, I will keep on singing your songs as I wash up!

David is small
David is small
David is beautiful
And David is small ...

I like talking to you in a silly voice, a baby David voice. It was lovely looking at your pictures today with Daddy. I studied your picture, first professional one taken in hospital – you look so sad, little Man of Sorrows. But Daddy led me to the ones in the living room – you with the sun hat on (He said you were seraphic I think – an angel) – you were a happy boy as well as a poorly boy weren't you? And the one taken in Sinnington, where you look so joyful. Thank you for your unconditional love, cheer, cheekiness, innocence, cuteness.

Sue Smith

A Way Forward

I'm not quite old enough to remember, as many do, where I was when I heard about the assassination of JFK but I can remember where I heard about Elvis's and Lennon's deaths. Now it is September 11 2001 that is forever etched in the memory of a generation. For me 9/11 is a very, very big personal memory too. While the world held its breath waiting for the inevitable collapse of the two towers, I was in a daze, floating in unreality, feeling euphoric and untouchable by events around me. I was in Woolworth's, choosing a present for my unborn baby. I was torn between two Winnie the Pooh sleepsuits … .decisions, decisions. I was vaguely aware of the newspaper vendor's cries outside, and knew that John had gone off to join the throng in Dixon's where all the TVs were tuned to this surreal and almost impossible window on the world. No one was bothered about buying a TV, staff waiting with baited breath too.

My 9/11

We were in Scarborough. We had just seen our consultant to discuss results of my 20-week scan. They had had what they called "a really good look" and everything seemed absolutely normal and I had been told to go away and enjoy the rest of my pregnancy. Hence the euphoria – we'd done it!! It had happened. We were going to be normal and have a normal baby *at last*. It had paid off, the gamble, the pushing our luck; the arrogance to think that after all we'd been through this *could* happen to us again. (The consultants, GP, midwives had been right – they had encouraged us to go for it, said we deserved another chance). Yes, it was September 2001. In November 1999 our first born son, David, had died, aged just 13 months. He had Down's Syndrome and a serious heart defect which, although initially surgery had corrected and contained, had meant he got progressively worse with each cold and chest infection. This eventually led to his death.

Even in the midst of Tuesday November 23 1999, when we held our dear son, still warm and peaceful but also so recently departed, I had said to John "We've got to have another baby" and he had replied "I know". In the anguish and grief of the following weeks and months a driving, determined voice grew louder inside me. Right, I'm going to be pregnant soon, definitely soon and I want to have a new baby in time for the first anniversary of David's death. Well, I was, then I wasn't and we didn't.

A Heartbeat

In July 2000, I discovered I was pregnant. Not surprisingly my menstrual cycle was erratic and it was not easy to tell. But a test confirmed suspicions. Yes! Punch the air! We'd done it! I'd wanted another baby, prayed for another baby and now there was going to be another baby, a baby to see me through the dark days ahead, the looming first anniversary of David's death, November 23 2000. This future would help me step away from the past. And the baby's name would be Grace (it had to be a little girl) and we would tell everyone that God's grace had been kind to us again and that weekend we happened to go to Mount Grace Priory and I sat on the grass picking daisies and smiling to myself with joy because it all *fitted*, it was all coming together again.

The next day was sunny. I was up early at the bottom of the garden with a mug of tea looking out over the sheep and fields with John. A sudden pain and a damp feeling. A subconscious "Oh my period's starting" then a conscious jolt of terror. Into the loo to see bloodied pants and a feeling of utter bewilderment. This wasn't part of the plan. To the GP, to the hospital, scan, we think you've miscarried early, can't see anything. A blood test to confirm. Some reassuring leaflets – it's very common, and after all you've been through ... A couple of days later, a 'phone call. Your pregnancy hormone levels in your blood are still a bit high, can you come back? Retest. Still high. You may be still pregnant – maybe it's too early to see on scan and your dates are so vague what with your erratic periods and some bleeding in early pregnancy isn't uncommon ... come in for another scan. Trying not to worry about the amount of alcohol I'd drunk in the last few days, I allowed my hopes to surface again. God, you're certainly leading us a merry dance but ok, here we go.

And then the horror, the second scan. Not just a miscarriage, but *this?* Pitchforked into another foul, evil, twisting pit of emotional, physical and spiritual blood and gore. "Mmm, yes, I've got a heartbeat". Yes! Spirits soar and fly once again. Then silence. Hushed whispers between the radiographer and midwife. "There's the ovary and then you see here ... " Then the brisk turning to me, holding my hand and explaining. It's an ectopic pregnancy. Your baby is growing in the wrong place. Can't possibly survive, must operate straight away. The world shrinks and collapses around me and John. Someone more important comes in and tells me it all again. Wheels begin to grind into motion – bed booked, theatre booked, they're going to operate this afternoon and I feel like a little frightened child again.

"I don't want an operation," I say

"But we need to make you better" they reply.

"But I don't feel poorly".

Then I'm terrified of the anaesthetic and signing a consent form to have a fallopian tube removed. I sign as long as they promise not to give me a hysterectomy as well. It's a nightmare; I'm so frightened and haunted by the fact they're going to remove something that has a heartbeat.

It happens. I survive. I come round. I'm in agony. Some silly cow of a nurse is there later to give me a bed bath and conversationally asks if I have any children. I want to kill her for not knowing about David and Grace.

The Clock's Slow Passage

So November 23 2000, David's first anniversary, finds us mourning two children; one known, one unknown. Still stunned and shell shocked from the past year, we revisit Leeds General Infirmary, where he died, look at his name in the Book of Remembrance and wonder whether it holds any meaning at all, but feeling this is as good a place as any to be right now.

How did we ever move on from there? Looking back, I really don't know – time passed. It helps, if not heals. We certainly had no plan, the determined voice driving me forward for a baby was subdued, not daring to speak, battered and beaten by bitter experience and harsh reality.

I was 36, I had one tube left and my eggs were either defective or incapable of getting to the right place. It was at this point, an incredibly low point, that the medics encouraged me that this *wasn't* the end of all hope, terribly unfortunate things had happened but the odds were in my favour and we should try again.

But that's how it felt to us. Life went on, time passed and I went back to work in September, two months after the ectopic pregnancy. A few days before the first anniversary of David's christening in October, I broke down at work and was signed off for a few weeks by my GP. Soon afterwards I developed pain and swelling in my foot which would not go away. Blood tests and x-rays did not reveal the problem and even a spell in hospital on intravenous antibiotics did not clear it up. It cleared up by itself eventually, never diagnosed and I returned to work after Christmas.

Looking back it seems that my body took control of what my mind wouldn't accept. My body decided I was pushing myself too hard and forced me to stop and, literally, put my feet up. There was no way I could work, and I didn't need to worry about the stigma of being signed off with depression. It's so much easier to be ill with a physical ailment. I remember long dull winter days sitting by the fire, reading, staring into space, watching the clock's slow passage until I could reasonably go to bed. It was a slow, gloomy, uneventful period but now I recognise it as a time when a lot of necessary mental healing and readjustment took place.

Back on my feet again, but still on antidepressants, patterns and structures began to reform. We continued jobs, went on holidays, bought things, made love, none of it with much hope or expectation but a bit of sunshine and laughter began to filter through.

The Tree of Knowledge

May 2001, and my period is late. A side effect of my ectopic operation is a clockwork menstrual cycle. I knew I had not allowed hope to die completely because I always knew when I was due, and could not entirely suppress the possibility that my period would not start. In May 2001 it didn't and once again I was pregnant. Astonishment, excitement and terror wrestled within me. Could I face all this again? To the GP and wheels start to turn once more. An early scan to check it's not ectopic again. No! Yippee! First hurdle over, but then I'm only at seven weeks and still have to get to twelve weeks plus before danger of miscarriage reduces.

John and I face hard decisions. Once we get to twelve weeks (with relief) some have to be made very quickly. Which tests would we like? There are many on offer. A nuchal fold scan checks the thickness at the back of the baby's neck at 11–14 weeks (it was a thickening at the back of David's neck, on a dating scan, that first alerted us to his Down's Syndrome). The triple blood test gives a probability of Down's Syndrome. Amniocentesis and chorionic villus sampling involve taking a sample of the fluid around the baby or cells from the placenta. These tell you for sure but carry a small risk of losing the baby. The temptation to *know* whether or not our baby has Down's Syndrome is very, very seductive. The desire so strong to pluck the apple from the tree of knowledge, to appease the serpent inside. But we wrestle. *Why* do we want to know? What will this knowledge give us? We don't want to terminate if the results are positive – *do we?* I tell myself we don't. Maybe it's more that living with a child with Down's Syndrome won't be as hard for me as it would be to live with having disposed of our less than perfect child. These are the same thoughts and arguments tumbling round and round that we had when we, unintentionally, found out about David.

But now there are other serpents writhing in this snake pit. I feel that going down the road of tests and knowledge is acknowledging and acquiescing to this recent tidal wave that says it is right for women to know about their unborn child, and indeed that all women will *want* to know. But it's not just the knowing is it? It's what to do with the knowledge, and for me the less palatable aspect of this search for knowledge and reassurance are the statistics that show most women finding out they have an unborn baby with Down's Syndrome choose to terminate the pregnancy. The tests and results are not just about being prepared for the future; they can literally be a matter of life and death. And it is this I feel reluctant to be a part of. But ... why am I still tempted?

I thought David had taught me that you couldn't classify babies as acceptable or not acceptable, suitable or unsuitable, wanted or unwanted. Even *considering* the tests seemed to give them worth, and that felt like a betrayal of David, of his memory, of children with Down's Syndrome and of all children with disabilities.

I knew that I would be terrified of the results and this I found hard to accept in myself.

Why was I scared? Scared of having another baby as wonderful as my little David? But I knew that deep down I had started to exercise my own prejudice. I had adored beyond measure my own son with Down's Syndrome but had met other babies and children with the same condition and secretly felt horror at the associated problems – autism, ADHD (attention deficit hyperactivity disorder), profound physical disabilities. I had been ashamed of the pride and relief that at least *my* baby wasn't *that* bad. What if now I *did* have one like that?

In the end we didn't have the nuchal fold scan, partly because our dithering meant we missed the optimum window of opportunity for it to work best, partly because of the cost! I *did* have the triple test, the results came back as 1 in 330, and no further testing is offered. (At 1 in 250 or less it is). I'd rather it was 1 in 10,000, as I know some friends have had, but it'll do. Then the dreadfully named anomaly scan is fine and the tidal wave of relief carries me to Woolworth's to agonise over which Winnie the Pooh sleepsuit to buy as the twin towers fall.

No Clear Path

What can I say or advise about moving on after a disabled child, after losing a child? Even now looking back I can discern no clear plan or pattern or pathway through it all, just tentative steps in certain directions rather than others. A lot of leaving to chance, to fate, or leaving doors ajar, just in case God wanted to act.

Now we have Matthew, born 7 February 2002, absolutely gorgeous, healthy and perfect. And, astonishingly, I am expecting a sister for him in November 2003 (due date 24 November, a day after David's fourth anniversary). Again, I am not quite sure how we got here. A seed settled in my heart and I began to wonder... Could we *possibly* try for another? For Matthew not to be by himself? To get another one in before I was 40? Or was I now being too arrogant and presumptuous, buoyed up with the success and joy of Matthew, pushing my luck even further? John wasn't sure, I was willing to go along with him. I could see the sense in being content with what we have, not risking more, putting ourselves through more anxiety and heartache not to mention exhaustion and sleepless nights again at our age. Then, amazingly, after just one night's "Oh what the hell, let's see what happens" I'm pregnant again. My goodness, that door was only *just* ajar. (I'm 39, one tube, still partially breastfeeding and I get pregnant after one try!).

Still very recent in our memories it all starts again and it is *no* easier. The tests, the choices. Not ectopic. Tick. Get to twelve weeks. Tick. Triple test 1 in 190. Sent into tailspin. The other side of 1 in 250 this time and the door opens to offers of an amniocentesis or chorionic villus sampling. Once again, after lots of dithering, wrestling, anxiety, sleeplessness and obsessive internet surfing, I decline. I try to gain control by looking at the statistics, trying to find the truth hidden there, but I know I'm looking in the wrong place. I imagine 190 women in a room. It would have to be a big room to fit us all in, a lecture theatre perhaps. Who has the baby with Down's Syndrome on her lap? Then I read that of women who get a "screen positive" (chance greater than 1 in 250), 1 in 60 go on to have a baby with disabilities. So does that mean my chances are 1 in 190 or 1 in 60 now? Consultant says still 1 in 190 but is he just being kind?

In the end I put my trust in the anomaly scan at 20 weeks, after one evening shouting "Damn it, I'm having this baby anyway and if it's anything like David what's the problem? What am I so scared of?" (I hasten to add that this was shouted with a little more bravado than I felt but desperately aware of my need to announce a decision, a position and stick to it).

Such A Fear of The Unknown

Once again the 20-week scan's "really good look" shows no markers or indicators of potential problems and relief floods us again. We see a consultant, a different one to usual, a few days later but I sense she's more cautious. She says yes everything looks fine but do bear in mind that babies with Down's Syndrome can "slip through" the net at this stage and go undetected. She chucks in the grenade that 1 in 3 babies with Down's Syndrome that are born have not shown abnormalities. Well I didn't know *that* before, in Woolies when the towers fell. John says later that she's just covering herself because I'm not having further tests and so I can't sue later. I console myself that the babies that slip through are ones without family history where the radiographer isn't as thorough as she's been with me ... and again feel the guilt and betrayal of David and his memory as I give in to this fear of disability once again. It's such a fear of the unknown. David was known and loved, this baby isn't known yet. That's what it is, not fear of a David, but fear of the unknown I tell myself. And that's where I am now. My baby is due in about eight weeks and all seems fine.

I have little time to think and dwell on the possibility of Down's Syndrome though I know the tiny chance is there. Common sense and peace reigns most of the time. 1 in 190 – well that's as near as dammit 1 in 200, which is 0.5 per cent, which is 99.5 per cent chance all is well ... But still there is that ache, that disappointment that feeling of betrayal of my firstborn, that I am frightened of having another baby like him. That despite all we have been through, the seismic shift in our world during the time we had him, I am still tainted with fear and prejudice, wanting normality and a "proper" baby. A realisation that he changed me but not as much as I would have liked. I have friends and acquaintances who are having babies and many have routinely forked out a couple of hundred quid for the nuchal fold scan. It seems a matter of course now, and not just for older "at risk" women. (I also hear on the news that the triple test is to be routinely offered to all pregnant women, not just those over 35). I chat to these women, who I like and respect, and feel odd, a freak, a misfit out of step when I mumble that I haven't had that test, that I've refused an amnio. I imagine their surprise, given my history. And I'm sucked in again, into the vortex, wondering whether I am being a fool, complacent, reckless. It gets hard to realise that I am not actually putting my baby at any risk whatsoever by not having these tests!

I talk to my mum and feel sad for the loss of innocence. Wistful for the time she describes when they didn't have scans or tests or scares. You didn't go to your doctor until you'd missed two periods and then you just got on with it and, probably, had your baby at home. But then, weren't they also the days when babies like my David were taken away and institutionalised, when you could be advised to leave them at the hospital and forget about them, when they wouldn't have been given anything like the chances he would have had?

I have no answers. My comfort is that I am beginning to accept that I probably never will and perhaps more importantly that I don't *need* to have them. I try to relax, to not be so hard on myself, to surrender to the flow, and accept the path I have been brought along rather than chosen. I try to accept that my fears are natural, and are actually separate from the love I have for David. I learn slowly that the fears can exist alongside the love without diminishing it.

Sue Smith

Four in the Morning

I'd forgotten
Woke at four
Saw it, saw locked door.

I woke and found him gone
His door is closed
No creaking bed
No breath of life
Just stillness
Awful standing stillness.

Libby Fletcher

Overwhelming Opportunities

Being the parent of any child is fraught with difficulties.
Being the mother of a child with extreme difficulties
is like having a volcano explode when you least expect it.
It was only when the word 'difficulty'
was exchanged for 'opportunity'
that my child became my most valuable opportunity.

These words were written on a day of overwhelming opportunity

A Mum

Silent Crying

Matthew is asleep in the car. He's my second child. Ordinary events can bring you up short, the day-to-day ambushes you and suddenly you are right back there, defenceless in the midst of it. Time has contracted, collapsed and I don't think I remember this until now. I can't bear to wake him so I leave him there while I have a coffee and a few minutes to myself. I pop out and peep every few minutes. He's so peaceful, safe, innocently angelic. Then the last time I go out he's just waking, stirring slowly and beginning to cry. He's alone and frightened but it's not that that floors me. I'm looking at him through a closed window, so I can't hear him. When my baby David had his heart surgery we sat by his bed in intensive care in Leeds. Suspended in time, cut off from this world, in another. Subterranean, too warm, too bright, but also eerily calm and peaceful. No responsibility, just watch and wait.

He was unconscious, drugged, wired, monitored and ventilated. He was also tiny, fragile, beautiful, innocent and lost within all the equipment. He had a big white dressing on his chest. I'd overheard things I didn't want to. I knew that under there his chest was still "open" – No, no, I didn't want to know that.

Why does the sight of my waking second son short circuit me right back to my intensively cared for first born? Well, when David began to come round he began to stir, in slow motion, gradually, and then he began to cry … but not cry. He was going through the motions, waving arms, crumpled face, head moving side-to-side but because of his ventilator tube in his throat his vocal cords could not produce the sound. A silent movie, surreal, unreachable, beyond. We could stroke him, touch him, but not lift him or cuddle him. He was saved by the life-blood of medicine and technology, guarded and protected but also imprisoned. My baby but not my baby, crying but not crying. And, unwittingly, just by being a baby, Matthew has transported me right back there. Past and present collide, clash like cymbals and I'm swimming through the heady concoction of real and remembered. Realities merge, making me high on the bitter-sweet drug of memories recaptured, the delight and overwhelming love for the baby that is here, wanting Mummy and dinner, and the achingly familiar pain for the baby that was, but isn't.

Sue Smith

I am Tom's Mother

Quarter to three in the morning
You're a hundred miles away
I haven't seen you for weeks.

I am not whole without you.
Whatever I do, wherever I am, I'm "Tom's mother".
Almost 19 but you need me now as much as you did the day we met.

I let James go but I'll never let go of you.
They tell me I have to:
When I die, you'll have to face the world without me.

Is this concept relevant to you?
Do you feel abandoned?
Does an hour seem like a day, a day like a week?

Without you I compartmentalise my days.
A bit of me for this, a bit of me for that
But in the middle of the night, only you.

You're coming home tomorrow, in truth you've never been away.
You're always here. I open your wardrobe and smell you on your clothes.
I open the fridge and there is a gap where your yoghurts should be.

Libby Fletcher

Just give me back my life

Just give me the key.
Which key? you ask.
Well, you said this was my home.
If it's my home,
Where's the bloody key?
Inside I'm just like you.
Heart but not body.
If my legs don't work
My brain still does,
At least for now.
So give me my key
My own bloody key.
You're here for me
Aren't you?
Then empower me with something
Soon I'll not be able to push a button
But for now give me my key.
For God's sake give me that bloody key
See it my way
So give me my key, not your key.
My Key
I need it now
Or what am I worth
When I am just ashes?
Just give me that key!
Is it too simple for you?
What did you say?
You'd like to give me
Something more condescending
Well, tough
All I want's that key
JUST GIVE ME THE BLOODY KEY

Libby Fletcher

Letting Go

It is almost 21 years since my youngest son was born, since I started to face the reality of his disabilities. Fears and anxieties have coloured my life for a very long time. What wouldn't I have given to know that the place I am in now existed and to know I would reach it one day? For a very long time, I was utterly convinced about two facts of life. First, that it was Tom and me against the world, and second, that there would be no life worth living for Tom without me there to care for and protect him. When your child is vulnerable the fear of abuse, in its many forms, is constant. To look to the future is painful.

You know how it is when an image stays with you through your life? Something can always trigger the image, in all its harsh reality. The image that haunted me was an elderly lady, shopping bag in one hand, and the other hand clutching that of her Mongol son. My son doesn't have Down's Syndrome but amongst his multiple disabilities he does have severe learning difficulties and needs constant supervision in public places. I foresaw a life of permanent attachment, a life of caring, nothing more, and nothing less.

I got on with life wearing a mask, a mask that hid my isolation, depression and exhaustion. The fog that descended upon me lifted occasionally when the actions and words of those with empathy and insight dispelled my misery and lifted the gloom. During Tom's toddler years the fog was fairly constant. I couldn't come to terms with my son's disabilities and the future seemed so bleak I hardly dare contemplate it. My mouth goes dry and the palpitations begin when I recollect that most difficult of times. My world was grey and I thought Tom's disabilities would colour my life, as well as his, for ever and ever. How wrong I was.

Letting Go of Anger

My isolation eased when Tom became a pupil at a very special school. Caring staff enabled me to reveal and dispel my fears, as Tom became part of a large and loving family. I will be eternally grateful to those who supported us when my reserves hit rock bottom. The respite their loving care afforded me enabled me to recharge my batteries. I coped. Every parent of a disabled child needs a coping strategy. And the best are those that help you to be open to those who offer a helping hand. If someone puts their arms around you and tells you it is ok to feel angry don't push them away and suppress your anger. If you do, your anger will lie dormant, a rumbling monster hell bent on destruction. It will finally erupt, as mine did, years later. I wish someone could have told me, in a way that I could understand, that my life would begin again when I let my anger go.

I'm preparing to finally cut the umbilical cord. Tom is moving on and relishing the prospect. I can see he will have a life worth living when I'm gone. That is such a comforting thought; it gives me an unbelievable peace. Facing my own mortality is no longer such a terrifying prospect. For 20 years, because I saw it only in the bleakest of light, I couldn't face the thought that Tom could live on without me. I now know he will. Amazing people have revealed that we all live under one sky. The colour has come back to my life. There is an extraordinary pleasure in the day as I rise and say "Thank you". I am letting go.

I will still be a huge part of Tom's life but I will no longer be defined as Tom's mother. The prospect of going back out into the world is daunting, exhilarating and liberating all at the same time. The optimism I feel for the future, for both Tom and myself, is overwhelming.

Peace of Mind

I woke early this morning. Last night I inadvertently set my alarm for 7am. I woke with a start, time to stir Tom and get him ready for college. Then came the realisation that he wasn't here, that someone else was waking him from slumber, coercing him into brushing his teeth, washing and getting dressed. I imagined him sitting on the stairs trying to tie the laces on his surgical boots. Would someone help him or would his laces trail and trip him up? Stop fretting, stop fretting. How long will it take to adjust to my new found freedom? Tom still lurks within the rhythm of my days and as the days move slowly on he is still beside me in my established routines.

Stop running, stop running, I must slow down the treadmill. I want to get off and rest awhile. I have bursts of energy and frantically attack the household chores, setting myself targets. Get Tom's room ready for Easter. His teddy is teetering on the edge of the shelf. It is still your home, Tom; your other home now.

My son is loving, caring and funny. How I miss him. He has so much to offer the community he moved to last week. I feel so blessed by those who are compelled to go the 'extra mile' for him, and for me.

There is a generosity of pocket and spirit, which has enabled Tom and myself to surface from the gloom into a bright future. When we were on the brink of Tom's move to a more independent way of life there was a lot of teetering on the edge. We held each other's hand as we made the leap into another life. I was hesitant. Tom was bold.

Tom has moved to Sutton Cottage, along with four young men with disparate disabilities. Their lives there are made possible by the Wilf Ward Trust, who manage and maintain the house enabling all five young men to enjoy a degree of independence within a secure and happy environment. This enables them to extend the boundaries of their world in a society which is becoming progressively more enlightened. Wilf Ward's vision has grown beyond his wildest dreams. His generosity and commitment enabled Tom and I to reach our own safe places, our own peace of mind. Some disabled children never live long enough to become young adults but for every disabled child who does, and for each and every parent of those children, there should be a Wilf Ward.

Libby Fletcher

9 A Suprisingly Positive Outcome

The Job of a Lifetime!

Summary of position

We are looking for a normal "it'll never happen to me" type person whose life we will turn upside down.

Essential skills include:

- Communication skills and report writing, often of a highly technical nature, and form filling
- Strong arms and back (for lifting, wheelchair pushing etc.)
- Light sleeper able to leap out of bed at the slightest noise, and clear up sick, diarrhoea etc. (without waking rest of household)
- Ability to ride emotional roller coaster
- Juggling while walking a tightrope a distinct advantage
- Ability to wear many different hats (quick changes often needed) and look convincing in all of them

The candidate should be able to:

- Show the necessary extraordinary cunning to secure adequate services for your child
- Suffer fools gladly, without ever displaying frustration
- Withstand child's distress during essential medical treatment (no candidate has satisfactorily fulfilled this requirement to date)
- Tolerate child's unusual behaviour / appearance
- Tolerate shortcomings of professionals, family, friends and strangers
- Appear cheerful at all times, especially when clinically depressed
- Applaud the achievements of other parents' offspring while secretly

praying that one day your child will write his name and be able to go to the toilet without you

The candidate will also have:

- Strong teeth (to grind or grit, as necessary)
- Intimate knowledge of the workings and financial management of public sector organisations (NHS, Education, Social Services)
- Detailed knowledge of the law as it relates to children, disability, education and medicine
- Experience of work in war zone (or similar situation)

Terms and Conditions

This position is suitable for: parents, key workers, peacemakers, warriors, educators, therapists, doctors, nurses, liaison officers, researchers, problem-solvers, engineers, mechanics, designers, diplomats, computer operators, advocates, cleaners, washerwomen, strongmen, plumbers (able to unblock toilets), builders (with knowledge of ramps), nutritionists, cooks, taxi or ambulance drivers, play leaders, care staff.

Preference will be given to individuals who are multi-skilled, in particular those who are able to change jobs quickly. The ideal person for this job would be able to perform all the above roles, and have experience of many environments.

The position is live-in, and the postholder will be on call 24 hours a day

Training

No initial training will be given and the postholder must use their initiative to access suitable training courses. Candidates should be prepared to undertake significant further study, as a commitment to lifelong learning is a pre-requisite of the job, but please note that learning will be done on the job and time off for study is not possible.

Support and line management arrangements

It is up to you to look for these if you so wish

Career prospects

Candidates may be able to hold down a second job, depending on their ability to find suitable cover for their primary responsibilities.

Please note: Candidates will take sole responsibility for establishing and maintaining this provision.

This is a permanent position and the successful applicant will be expected to sign a contract for life.

Pay

Carer's allowance and child benefit.

There are no sickness benefits in place.

There is no pension scheme.

There are no paid holidays.

There is no union representation.

There is no occupational health scheme.

There are no maternity benefits or arrangements.

There is no opportunity for early retirement.

We are an equal opportunities employer and welcome applicants regardless of class, ethnic background, religion, sexuality or disability.

Opportunities for personal development

Applicants are advised that they may be surprised at the direction their life takes following their appointment.

Previous applicants have advised us that there have been unexpected benefits such as:

- Surprising joy and laughter
- A realigning of personal perspectives
- Falling in love with your child.

We take no responsibility for the above.

A Gentler Way

Hal sits on the sofa. The room is in chaos, full of the incongruous objects which rise to the surface in a house move. He gazes intently at the television screen, then with equal intensity at his right hand. With delicate fingers he makes patterns of mathematical precision. He separates one finger from the rest, then two, then three, widening the angle each time. I can't do this. He loves the finger song *'Tommy Thumb, Tommy Thumb where are you? / Here I am, Here I am. How do you do?'*

Accept What Is

His fingers are long, slender, flexible. If things were different he might have been a musician or a painter. It is hard to put such thoughts aside, reject what might have been and accept what is.

Hal has required me to slow down and watch and listen. He has asked me to abandon ordinary aspiration and ordinary ambition and learn to sit still and wait. He has a kind of sixth sense about people, warms to decent, kindly people. Intuition and empathy are his peculiar gifts. He acts as a magnet for exactly those people who he needs to know and who need to know him. His wonder and pleasure often exceeds that of other children. Hal needs as much attention as a lover. He requires that level of intensity, the electricity of focused concentration.

I have often resented his slow, measured world of being. I find it painful to slow from the furious pace of an argument or an essay, where it is good to sparkle and kindle, to the slow spooning of food, the laborious routine of physiotherapy exercises, the repetitive actions of caring. I am afraid that I might sink completely and be lost.

Teach Me Tenderness

He reminds me of my own finiteness and of the infirmity and temporary nature of my physical ability. Hal is teaching me tenderness for what is weak, vulnerable and dependant in myself. This slowing down of time has been important for me too. I needed time to contemplate and meditate. I needed to resist the temptation to fix the problem. I needed to learn how to be with this life which was now mine as well as his. But Hal also demonstrates the vitality of spirit in the shell of the body and embodies the profound understanding of so many faiths, that what is most real about us humans is something other than body.

I had to try to make sense of innocent suffering. Because however much we may talk positively about disability there is the inescapable fact that something has got to be undergone, suffered, by this child of mine. I don't want to slip into that facile dramatisation of a disabled person's life 'from tragedy to triumph'. Nor do I want to celebrate the positive outcomes of Hal's disability, or rejoice in the enlightenment he has brought me, the martyr mother of a disabled child.

Dream the Dream

I used to have two recurring dreams about Hal.

In the first I am sitting doing something quite ordinary, washing up perhaps, or sitting reading, and Hal comes walking into the room. Or sometimes he runs in. And I tell myself – quite irritably – 'There you see – he was fine all along – why were you so worried?'

In the second, I have just put him into the bath, then I am suddenly distracted by something, the telephone, a pan on the stove, and I leave him just for a moment. When I come back, he is dead, lying pale and lumpen under the water.

Recently I read a psychologist's account of the experiences and psychological 'events' which parents of disabled children undergo. The families of disabled children are a source of consuming interest to psychologists. There are many articles which analyse the processes by which we hear of our children's disability, react and finally come to terms with our situation. I suppose the psychologist would interpret my first dream as a denial fantasy, and the second as guilt and fear of my great responsibility. Even if the psychologist is right, her dark and gloomy vision is not much help to me as I learn to live with Hal's disability. I prefer to think of the first dream as a dream of hope. Not of course of false hope. Notwithstanding a miracle, Hal won't ever run, or even walk, into the room to find me. But my dreaming mind has found an image with which to embody my hope for Hal. My imagination has produced not a fantastic, but an everyday image of wholeness. A little boy runs into the room. This is not denial, but the truth. Every day, Hal comes home from school, giggling and babbling and wriggling in his wheelchair. My dream world has supplied the body for his running, leaping spirit.

Walk a Tightrope

I was once at a conference where the audience (social workers mostly) were discussing what it was like being the parent of a disabled child. “It’s a bereavement,” said one, very knowledgeably. “Parents grieve for the child they didn’t have and the grief process just goes on and on”. I asked for the microphone. “Actually it’s not much like bereavement,” I said. “It’s more like having a child. Diagnosis is a shock, but then you just get on with it. You live through the ups and downs just like any other family”.

Psychologizing us – analysing our ‘denial’, ‘anger’ and ‘acceptance’ seems to me a way of distancing themselves from the pain of the situation. Is grief easier to bear because psychologists have enumerated the four stages of grieving? Are there people with four star grieving processes? It sometimes feels like that as a parent. People even congratulate you on how well you’re doing. I am impatient with those who ‘understand what I’m going through’ and I am drawn to those who understand what is happening to me because they recognise it. They are not theorists who distance pain, but authentic living people who have faced difficulty and lived through it.

This experience is like walking on a tightrope. On one side is my fear of losing Hal – the threats posed by surgery, by fits, by bouts of illness. In special schools, among the families you know, death of children can become terribly commonplace. Facing this and finding a way to live with it. Praying, willing, helping your child through illness, surgery and vulnerability requires immense expenditure of energy. On the other side is the fear of a blank, bleak future, my own life half-lived, hopes unfulfilled. The second vision has become less fearful with the passage of time, as my experience deepens, but that means the first fear becomes more intense. Bound in also is the taboo around us and our families. Even today when the world supposes itself to be rational and scientific, I have experienced a superstitious rejection and distancing. Not always, not everywhere, but distinct and frequent enough to be noticeable. We live with what every parent-to-be fears and confound the antenatal mantra ‘I don’t care if it’s a boy or a girl – so long as it’s healthy’. That’s a strange thing.

Confronting the fear, travelling to the unknown land releases a superb burst of creative energy and a burning need to make sense of it all. That is what they mean when they tell you how rewarding it is.

Gillian Upton Holmes

The Contributors

Anonymous sent her work to the group through a friend.

A Mum is very proud of her amazing children and shall be eternally grateful to them for being her inspirational teachers and bringing so much worth and overwhelming love into the world. These are her words, make of them what you will.

A Young Person just wants to be herself and not included in work because of her disability.

Lesley is an ex-nurse and midwife, a single parent and a very committed and caring mother. Her aims now are (still) to discover the 'meaning of life', to support all her children as best she can, to grow and develop in all areas with an open mind.

Libby Fletcher is Chairman of Ryedale Special Families and the mother of two very special sons who have now flown the nest. She lives with migraine and clinical depression, finding solace and inspiration when riding her horse, Poppy, through Dalby forest. She yearns to be a free spirit, dares to dream and is now putting pen to paper with a vengeance. Working on this book has reawakened her passion for writing poetry, which she is finding both healing and stimulating.

Rebecca O'Rourke is a writer and an adult educator. Her understanding of disability was limited before she volunteered to support the writing project at RSF. Working on the book has enabled her to challenge her assumptions about disability and gain a greater knowledge and insight into the common, and complex, experience of living with disability.

Gillian Payne is a trustee of Ryedale Special Families, whose writing had previously taken the form of professional reports connected with her work as a Speech and Language Therapist. She is the mother of two sons and a daughter, each of whom has taught her a great deal in their journey to adulthood. Working on this book has sometimes been unsettling and sometimes rewarding but ultimately it has been a positive experience.

Heidi Ridgewell is a 30-year old mother of Charlie. Charlie was her first child, born 12 weeks prematurely. She always believed that he would exceed professional expectations and wrote her diary to pass the time and to read back to him when he could understand just how far he had travelled. She feels she has also travelled a long way to where she is now, in being far more educated, fortunate and above all, blessed. Working on this book has inspired her to begin a creative writing course with the Open University.

John Smith is the proud father of David, Matthew and Ruth. He was a secondary school history teacher for many years before starting to train teachers. Shortly after changing career, his son, David, was born. He has always enjoyed writing and his work ranges from academic books and journals to children's stories and plays.

Sue Smith is a physics teacher (the best bits are teaching students that the universe is made of quarks named truth and beauty), wife to John and mum to David, Matthew and Ruth. She has often found writing a release for pain and confusion and this writing project was very welcome after the death of her firstborn son David. Working on the book, especially the chat, laughter and friendship it generated, has been a significant part of her bereavement journey, which also saw the birth of her second son Matthew and daughter Ruth.

When **Gillian Upton Holmes**' son Hal was born with severe disabilities in 1993, she did not anticipate her own re-birth as a warrior parent. She has been to more meetings, consultations and conferences about giving support to disabled children and their families than she can count and has become increasingly intolerant of talk without effective action. More than ten years of active service, including periods as a trustee of the Family Fund and chairman of Ryedale Special Families, have granted her insights about the various barriers which disabled children face. Gradually she has learned the importance of patient, determined persistence, to bite her tongue and to never, ever despair. She remains hopeful about the future for Hal and children like him. Working on this project has confirmed her hunch that the process of developing the book, as well as the book itself, would be invaluable in establishing the sense of self and purpose needed by parents of disabled children.

Ryedale Special Families

Writing and publishing *Altered Images* has been a voluntary project, supported by Ryedale Special Families. Ryedale Special Families, established in 1997, is a parent-led charity which supports the parents of children with special needs, disability or an illness in the largely rural area of Ryedale, North Yorkshire.

Ryedale Special Families
121 Town Street
Old Malton
Malton
North Yorkshire YO17 7HD
Telephone: 01653 699000
Fax: 01653 690198
E-mail: post@ryedalespecialfamilies.fsnet.co.uk

Additional Resources

Information about support groups and other resources for parents of children with disabilities and special educational needs changes so rapidly that we decided not to include it in this publication. Up-to-date information about support groups, campaigns and other resources can be accessed through your local library, the Citizen's Advice Bureau or your local Carer's Centre, details of which will be available from your GP.